CHOICES

GEOPOLITICS IN THE 21ST CENTURY

For a quarter century since the fall of the Berlin Wall, the world has enjoyed an era of deepening global interdependence, characterized by the absence of the threat of great power war, spreading democracy, and declining levels of conflict and poverty. Now, much of that is at risk as the regional order in the Middle East unravels, the security architecture in Europe is again under threat, and great power tensions loom in Asia.

The Geopolitics in the 21st Century series, published under the auspices of the Order from Chaos project at Brookings, will analyze the major dynamics at play and offer ideas and strategies to guide critical countries and key leaders on how they should act to preserve and renovate the established international order to secure peace and prosperity for another generation.

CHOICES

INSIDE THE MAKING OF
INDIA'S FOREIGN POLICY

SHIVSHANKAR MENON

Brookings Institution Press
Washington, D.C.

Copyright © 2016
THE BROOKINGS INSTITUTION
1775 Massachusetts Avenue, N.W., Washington, D.C. 20036
www.brookings.edu

Library of Congress Cataloging-in-Publication data

Names: Menon, Shivshankar, 1949– author.
Title: Choices : inside the making of India's foreign policy /
    Shivshankar Menon.
Description: Washington, D.C. : Brookings Institution Press,
    2016. | Includes bibliographical references and index.
Identifiers: LCCN 2016030037 (print) | LCCN 2016036378
    (ebook) | ISBN 9780815729105 (pbk. : alk. paper) |
    ISBN 9780815729112 (ebook)
Subjects: LCSH: India—Foreign relations—21st century. |
    India—Foreign Relations—1984–
Classification: LCC DS449 .M46 2016 (print) | LCC DS449
    (ebook) | DDC 327.54—dc23
LC record available at https://lccn.loc.gov/2016030037

9 8 7 6 5 4 3 2 1

Typeset in Sabon and Scala Sans

Composition by Westchester Publishing Services

Contents

List of Maps

Acknowledgments

THE SEED OF THIS BOOK was planted in a study group on Indian foreign policy at Harvard University's Kennedy School in the cold spring of 2015. I am grateful to Nick Burns and Graham Alison at Harvard University, to Richard Samuels at MIT, and to Strobe Talbott and Martin Indyk at the Brookings Institution, who made it possible for me to spend time on this project.

Thanks are also due to friends who were good enough to read and comment on the manuscript in its various shape-shifting versions—you know who you are, and I shall not shame you by naming you.

Without Ranjana Sengupta's eagle eye, ideas, and editing, this would be a much poorer book. Valentina Kalk and Bill Finan at the Brookings Institution Press, and Angela Piliouras, made publishing a book easy for a first-time author. They are not responsible for what follows.

But most of all I am grateful to Mohini, without whom not just the book but life itself would not mean anything.

Introduction

ALL GOVERNMENTS CLAIM ETERNAL consistency and success. Some even claim omniscience. And yet the essence of governance is choice. Choice involves uncertainty, risk, and immediacy; those who must make the choices operate in the contemporary fog that envelops events rather than from the certainty and clarity that come with time, distance, and reflection. Nowhere is this more true than in foreign policy decisionmaking. Diplomacy offers choices, and those choices must be negotiated with other sovereign actors not subject to a particular state's customs, laws, and restraints.

The chapters that follow explore five instances in which the Indian state made choices and entered into negotiations with long-term implications for India's foreign policy. They examine the options that were available at the time, why the choices were made in the way they were, and the consequences of those choices. But the reader should be aware that these five instances are neither a complete nor necessarily an archetypical set of choices; rather, they were selected because they were the ones with which I was directly associated.

MY GENERATION OF INDIAN diplomats was blessed in many ways. Born free Indians, educated and trained in independent India, and having joined the Indian Foreign Service in the heady days after victory in the India-Pakistan War of 1971, we have seen India transformed before our eyes. As India grew its economy and accumulated power, it gained agency in the international system, its options increased, and the scope and significance of the choices it made steadily expanded. We may have been uniquely blessed. As practice and precedent continue to accumulate, thence to harden into bureaucratic carapace, and as foreign and security policymaking in India becomes more institutionalized, opportunities for radical change, individual initiative, and innovation will diminish. Future generations of Indian diplomats are unlikely to enjoy the freedom of action and choice that the cohort with which I trained and worked did, except in times of great turmoil and upheaval.

I had the good fortune to be associated with or to participate in the events surrounding the foreign policy choices discussed here, either in the Ministry of External Affairs in New Delhi or as foreign secretary and then national security adviser to the prime minister between 2006 and 2014; earlier I had served as ambassador or high commissioner to China, Pakistan, Sri Lanka, and Israel. Seven years working with the Atomic Energy Commission in Mumbai and in Vienna also contributed to an interest in the politics and diplomacy of atomic energy.

These choices relate to the post–Cold War period, when the certainties of a bipolar world had been replaced by the unipolar moment, with the United States as the sole superpower; when the rise of China was evident but not yet certain; and when each of India's neighbors was undergoing significant transitions. Many of us argued at the time that the end of the Cold War had opened up opportunities for Indian foreign and security policies to break through previously hard ideological and alliance barriers. India itself was very different from the India that had gained independence in 1947, when the average life expectancy was twenty-six years, only about one-seventh of the population was literate, and there had been half a century of near zero growth in the economy under empire. After independence, India's steady, if slow, accumulation of economic power and social change was accompanied, particularly after the growth spurt of the 1980s, by the beginning of the accumulation of hard power capabilities. India's army had been honed by four wars, including one ending in defeat; the navy was beginning to venture out of coastal waters; and nuclear weapons capabilities and options had been preserved and built up.

By the mid-1990s, middle-class Indian citizens' faith in India's future as a great power was buttressed by a realistic prospect of how this could come about. India was changing at an unprecedented rate and in ways that were scarcely imaginable when my generation entered the Foreign Service in the early 1970s. The economic crisis of 1990–91 enabled

India's leadership to break with the domestic economic and political certainties of the past and brought a new leadership to power, P. V. Narasimha Rao and Manmohan Singh. Reforms, such as dismantling the crippling set of government regulations known as the licence-permit system, and opening India to the world from 1991 on, saw a series of actions that coincided with the high noon of the globalized world economy between 1989 and 2008. India was a major beneficiary, second only to China, of the free flows of trade and capital and the relatively open markets of the global economy at that time.

The architects and implementers of the post-1991 liberalization and reform in India, P. V. Narasimha Rao and Manmohan Singh, were also present and future prime ministers who, along with Prime Minister Atal Bihari Vajpayee, oversaw the adjustment of India's foreign and security policies to this brave new post–Cold War world. All three, Rao, Vajpayee, and Singh, had thought deeply about foreign policy before entering office, and all brought abundant intellectual capital to the task of remaking India's policies to fit the changed situation. Rao and Vajpayee had been foreign ministers, while Singh's international experience and analytical bent of mind enabled him to take office with clear ideas of what was needed. One need only look at the clarity of the path Singh outlined to Jonathan Power of the *New York Times* in the week he assumed office,[1] when he anticipated the major lines of India's policies over the next ten years. Rao, Vajpayee, and Singh were intellectuals who enjoyed playing with the concepts, ideas, and options that new foreign policy challenges posed, as was Jaswant Singh, Vajpayee's foreign minister in critical periods of Vajpayee's administration.

They also shared an unanticipated—and largely underestimated—ability and determination to see through their initiatives, despite the fragile political foundations of their governments: a minority government for Rao and a fractious party and coalition for Vajpayee and Singh. How they did so was an education. Narasimha Rao, with his reputation as the *Chanakya*[2] of Indian politics, used crisis to reform the economy and consultation to ease through the Border Peace and Tranquility Agreement with China. Atal Bihari Vajpayee single-handedly used his powers of persuasion to make the idea of the United States as an ally acceptable in India, to engage with Pakistan despite cross-border terrorism, and to make India a declared nuclear weapon state. Manmohan Singh, reputedly gentle, staked his own prime ministership and the future of his first government on getting the civil nuclear initiative with the United States through India's Parliament by political maneuvering that Chanakya himself would have envied. There was remarkable continuity in policy among these three prime ministers, with each building on his predecessor's work and all acknowledging each other's contributions.

TAKEN TOGETHER, THE CHOICES considered in this book reveal certain predilections in Indian foreign policy across governments irrespective of their political hues. I hesitate to call this India's strategic culture because both the term itself and its definition have occasioned so much debate. If India does convert its weight and influence into becoming a great power, as its present trajectory suggests, it is these predilections that will determine the kind of great power it will be.

My aim is not to write a history or to examine counterfactuals except insofar as they influenced the decisions. Rather, I have attempted to describe, as honestly as possible, the reasons and considerations that weighed in the choices that were made in government, on behalf of India. That some choices were controversial, and remain so, is in the nature of such decisions. Public argument is part of the process of democratic discussion to which foreign policy must be subject, even though diplomacy remains a private, esoteric, and remote art in its essential core practice.

The decisions examined here cover India's relationships with the United States, China, Pakistan, and Sri Lanka, and India's nuclear posture. They relate to a period when India's engagement with the world was redrawn: when relations with the United States were transformed, relations with China were stabilized (though whether they will stay so is an open question), the neighborhood was integrated, and serious attempts were made to resolve long-standing issues with Pakistan and others. In some of these choices the moment of transition, of a phase change in policy, is clear. The fact that the policies represented by these choices have been continued by the successor government suggests that the shifts they represent have now been internalized, absorbed into the practice of Indian foreign policy and the common understanding of what India's interests are. India's global role and posture are still largely the result of these and similar choices; hence their lasting significance.

WITH RESPECT TO THE structure of the book, the chapters are arranged in chronological order. The first explores the 1993 decision by the Narasimha Rao government to obtain a legal Chinese commitment to maintain the status quo on the India-China border. To do so within thirty years of the 1962 conflict when Parliament had pledged to recover every inch of Indian territory required both skilled domestic political management and complex negotiations with the Chinese government.

Chapter 2 describes the choices involved in the Civil Nuclear Initiative with the United States, when Prime Minister Manmohan Singh removed the major obstacle to an India-U.S. partnership, staking the fate of his government on a no-confidence vote in Parliament, the only instance in India of a government's fate being pegged to a foreign policy issue.

Chapter 3 examines India's decision not to respond with overt force to the mass casualty terrorist attack on Mumbai on November 26, 2008, by Lashkar-e-Taiba terrorists from Pakistan, who clearly had support from the Pakistan intelligence agency (the ISI) and the Pakistan Army. The chapter raises issues of India's use of force and the more general question of the limited utility of force against nonstate actors and terrorists who enjoy state support.

Chapter 4 deals with India's choices in the closing phases of the Sri Lankan civil war in early 2009, when Sri Lanka used military force to successfully eliminate the Liberation Tigers of Tamil Eelam (LTTE) as a fighting force. India had to choose between its humanitarian concerns and domestic political imperatives, which called for measures to protect the Tamil population in northern Sri Lanka, and its strategic interest in maintaining good relations with the Sri Lankan government in Colombo. In the event, India had to balance these interests and walk a fine policy line, the success or failure of which is still debated in India.

Chapter 5 examines why India has nuclear weapons but is also one of the few nuclear weapon states to pledge not to use them first against another state.

The final chapter attempts to elicit from the experience of decision-making in these several instances a sense of how India has gone about its foreign and security policymaking and of the predilections and worldview its choices reveal. India's inclinations should become even more significant in the future as the nation stays on course to become a modern, prosperous, and strong state, a great power in the family of nations.

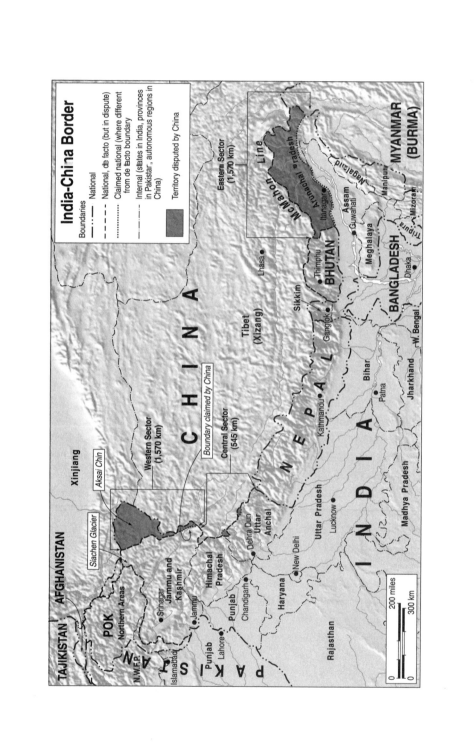

India-China Border

Boundaries

- – – · – – National
- – – – – National, de facto (but in dispute)
- ·········· Claimed national (where different from de facto boundary)
- – – – – – Internal (states in India, provinces in Pakistar., autonomous regions in China)

▨ Territory disputed by China

TAJIKISTAN

AFGHANISTAN

Xinjiang

POK

Northern Areas

N.W.F.P.

Siachen Glacier

Aksai Chin

Srinagar

Jammu and Kashmir

Jammu

Islamabad

Lahore

Punjab

Punjab

Chandigarh

Himachal Pradesh

Haryana

New Delhi

Dehra Dun

Uttar Anchal

Rajasthan

Uttar Pradesh

Lucknow

Western Sector (1,570 km)

Boundary claimed by China

Central Sector (545 km)

C H I N A

Tibet (Xizang)

Lhasa

Kathmandu

N E P A L

Sikkim

Gangtok

Bihar

Patna

Jharkhand

Madhya Pradesh

I N D I A

BHUTAN

Thimphu

Eastern Sector (1,570 km)

McMahon Line

Arunachal Pradesh

Itanagar

Assam

Guwahati

Nagaland

Manipur

Meghalaya

BANGLADESH

Dhaka

Tripura

Mizoram

W. Bengal

MYANMAR (BURMA)

P A K I S T A N

200 miles

300 km

0

0

CHAPTER ONE

Pacifying the Border

The 1993 Border Peace and
Tranquility Agreement with China

> The basis of government is jugglery. If it works, and lasts, it becomes policy.
> —A wazir in ninth-century Baghdad

IN APRIL 1992, Foreign Secretary Jyotindra Nath Dixit asked me whether it was possible for India to settle its dispute with China over the boundary. He was accompanying Prime Minister P. V. Narasimha Rao on a visit to Japan, where I was stationed. Secretary Dixit also posed the question of what India and China could do with their relationship.

I had come to Japan in late 1989 from a second posting in Beijing, having dealt with China off and on for more than eight years. I had wandered into the Foreign Service as a means to see China before returning to attempt a PhD thesis on ancient Indian and Chinese kingship. In the early 1970s an Indian could see China in one of two ways: as an underground Maoist guerrilla or as a diplomat. I chose the easier course. Once inside the Foreign Service, I enjoyed working as a diplomat too much to leave. Dixit knew this background when he posed his question.

I rashly volunteered that settling the boundary seemed unlikely at that time because the gap in positions was too wide, but that China might be ready to agree to steps to maintain peace along the border based on the present status quo. Dixit asked why I thought so. I noted that the Tiananmen Square trauma was still fresh in the minds of the Chinese leadership under Deng Xiaoping. Military force had been used in June

1989 in the heart of China's capital city against the Chinese people, who were demonstrating for democracy and freedom and had occupied the area for more than two months. The Tiananmen Square incident had also revealed deep divisions within the Chinese leadership. Besides, having watched the Soviet Union collapse, and concerned that China was next on the U.S. list of targets for regime change, the Chinese leadership could not make territorial concessions, which the Chinese people would see as weakness. But the same fears should make the leadership willing to ensure peace along the border with India, freeing the Chinese government to deal with more pressing concerns of internal stabilization and the United States. Later during the visit Secretary Dixit asked me to repeat to the prime minister what I had told him. Prime Minister Rao listened, thought, pouted, and said he would talk to us again in Delhi.

No good deed goes unpunished in government. By July 1992 my cocky opinions had landed me in the Ministry of External Affairs in Delhi as joint secretary for North and East Asia, dealing with China, Mongolia, Taiwan, Nepal, Bhutan, and Tibet. Secretary Dixit and Prime Minister Rao thought we should try to implement the idea of consolidating peace and tranquility along the border. Dixit had already mentioned the idea to China's then vice foreign minister, Tang Jiaxuan, after our initial conversation. The Chinese had sounded interested but noncommittal.

In essence, we proposed using the distinction between the boundary, which was disputed, and the border, or the status quo, on which we wanted to maintain the peace. Although colloquially the terms tend to be used interchangeably, a boundary is the line between two states that marks the limits of sovereign jurisdiction. In other words, a boundary is a line agreed upon by both states and normally delineated on maps and demarcated on the ground by both states. A border, on the other hand, is a zone between two states, nations, or civilizations. It is frequently also an area where peoples, nations, and cultures intermingle and are in contact with one another.

India has consistently believed and maintained that there is a traditional customary boundary between India and Tibet, one that also is formalized by legal agreements for most of its length, including those covering the McMahon Line, agreed to by Great Britain, China, and Tibet at the 1914 Simla Conference; in the eastern sector the Tibet-Sikkim boundary along the watershed of the Teesta–Amochu rivers, agreed to formally in the Anglo-Chinese Convention of 1906 affirming the Anglo-Tibetan Convention of 1904 (which also introduced Chinese suzerainty

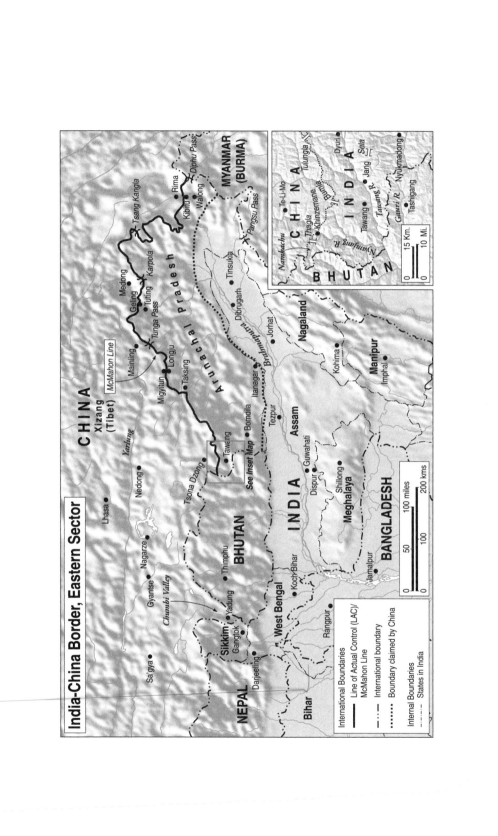

India-China Border, Eastern Sector

CHINA
Xizang
(Tibet)

Lhasa

Nedong

Nagarze

Gyantse

Sa'gya

Chumbi Valley

Yadung

Gangtok

Darjeeling

Thimphu

BHUTAN

Sikkim

NEPAL

Bihar

West Bengal

Koch Bihar

Rangpur

Jamalpur

BANGLADESH

Meghalaya

Shillong

Dispur

Guwahati

INDIA

Assam

Tezpur

Bomdila

Tawang

Tsona Dzong

See Inset Map

Itanagar

Taksing

Longju

Migyitun

Mainling

Tunga Pass

Tuting Pass

Geling

Medong

Karpola

Tsang Kangla

Rima

Kibithu

Walong

Diphu Pass

Pangsu Pass

Yarlung

Arunachal Pradesh

Brahmaputra

Tinsukia

Dibrugarh

Jorhat

Nagaland

Kohima

Manipur

Imphal

MYANMAR
(BURMA)

McMahon Line

International Boundaries
—— Line of Actual Control (LAC)/
McMahon Line
–··– International boundary
········ Boundary claimed by China

Internal Boundaries
–··– States in India

0   50   100 miles
0   100   200 kms

Inset Map

CHINA

Namkachu

Te-Li-Mo

Thagla

Khinzemane

Bumla

Tulungla

Dyuri

Sela

Jang

Nyukmadong

Tashigang

Tawang

Nyamjang R.

Tawang R.

Gauri R.

INDIA

BHUTAN

0   15 Km.
0   10 Mi.

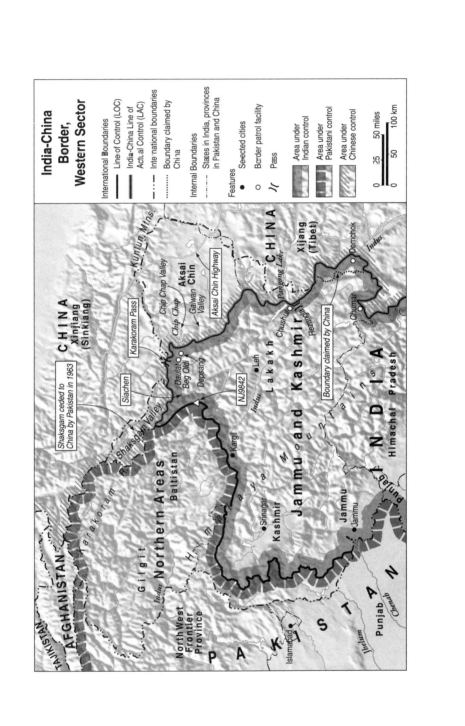

India-China
Border,
Western Sector

International Boundaries
——— Line of Control (LOC)
——— India-China Line of
        Actual Control (LAC)
–··– International boundaries
········ Boundary claimed by
        China

Internal Boundaries
–··– States in India, provinces
        in Pakistan and China

Features
● Selected cities
○ Border patrol facility
)(Pass

Area under
Indian control

Area under
Pakistani control

Area under
Chinese control

0   25   50 miles
0   50   100 km

CHINA
Xinjiang
(Sinkiang)

Kunlun Mtns.

Shaksgam ceded to
China by Pakistan in 1963

Karakoram Pass

Chip Chap Valley

Chip Chap

Aksai Chin

Galwan Chin
Valley

Aksai Chin Highway

Siachen

Karakoram

Shaksgam Valley

Daulat
Beg Oldi

Depsang

NJ9842

CHINA

Xijiang
(Tibet)

Pangong Lake

Chushul

Rezang la

Demchok

Indus

Chumar

Boundary claimed by China

●Leh

Indus

Ladakh

Gilgit

Northern Areas

Baltistan

Himalaya

●Kargil

Jammu and Kashmir

Karakoram

Indus

North West
Frontier
Province

●Srinagar

Kashmir

Karakoram

INDIA

Himachal Pradesh

Jammu

●Jammu

TAJIKISTAN

AFGHANISTAN

●Islamabad

PAKISTAN

Punjab

Jhelum

Chenab

Ravi

Beas

over Tibet); and various lines agreed to by Tibetan governments with the rulers of Jammu and Kashmir state and Himachal from the seventeenth century on.[1]

When the Chinese People's Liberation Army (PLA) moved into Tibet in 1950, for the first time in history the Chinese government had a permanent military presence on the border with India. Previous Chinese military and political involvement in Tibet and reprisal raids on the Gorkha kings in Nepal in the eighteenth century, during the Qing emperor Qian Long's time, had used local troops and were relatively brief. In fact, when the Gorkha kings tried to involve the Chinese in their quarrels with rising British power on the Indian subcontinent in the late eighteenth and early nineteenth centuries, before the First Opium War of 1839–42, it was settled Chinese imperial policy to refrain from sending supplies, funds, or troops and to avoid entanglement, as was made clear in repeated edicts by successive Qing dynasty emperors.[2]

After 1950, when India made its view on the boundary clear, the Chinese did not demur. In 1954 and 1956 Nehru raised the matter of Chinese activity on what was considered the Indian side of the boundary and of the incorrect Chinese maps, and Premier Zhou Enlai responded that those were old Kuomintang maps and that the Chinese were looking into the matter. Zhou assured Nehru that China had no claims on Indian territory.[3] Indeed, the 1954 Agreement on Trade and Intercourse between India and the Tibet Region of China included specific mention of several passes that would be used for border trade, which seemed to confirm the Indian view. (It was only in 1960 that China argued that mentioning mountain passes for border trade did not mean that they were actually boundary passes.)

In January 1959 Zhou first made it clear in writing that China disputed the McMahon Line in the eastern sector and the Kunlun boundary in the western sector, and said that China wanted to negotiate the entire India-China boundary line.[4] The McMahon Line was described as an illegal vestige of colonialism. But in practice, China accepted the same line by another name as the boundary with Burma in 1960. And in 1960 Zhou Enlai came to Delhi and suggested to Prime Minister Jawaharlal Nehru that China might accept the McMahon Line as the boundary in the east if India accepted the status quo created in the west by China moving forward into Aksai Chin during the 1950s—though India still claimed Aksai Chin as its own territory. Nehru and Indian public opinion were outraged that China was effectively taking over Indian territory through cartographic aggression and by changing facts on the ground militarily, building the Aksai Chin road from Sinkiang to Tibet and garrisoning the area in the mid-1950s. To the Chinese, the timing of India's rejection of their offer, soon after India had given asylum to the Dalai Lama in March 1959, seemed to confirm their belief that India had designs on Tibet, which was in full-fledged revolt against Beijing's rule at that time. The Chinese were convinced that the guerrilla war in Tibet from the mid-1950s to the early 1970s was aided and made possible by the CIA and Indian agencies.

For India, on the other hand, it was bad enough that the British Empire for imperial reasons had sacrificed Indian interests in Tibet at the 1914 Simla Conference, including agreeing to the McMahon Line and handing over Tibet to China to keep the Russians out. Now the Chinese were demanding even more than the gift given them by the British.

In 1962 the world's largest boundary dispute, involving more than 120,000 square miles of territory, led to war in the high Himalayas. (Strictly speaking, neither side formally declared war—the reason it is referred to as a conflict.) On October 20, China attacked isolated Indian posts that had been established to show the flag and prevent further Chinese incursions into Indian territory in both eastern and western sectors. The war was fought in two phases, in October and November. In effect, the Chinese were held at Walong near the Myanmar tri-junction. Near Tawang, beside the eastern tri-junction with Bhutan, the Chinese PLA inflicted a psychologically damaging and politically traumatic rout on Indian forces. In the western sector fighting was fierce at Rezangla and near Chushul, in Jammu and Kashmir state. Chinese troops cleared all Indian posts on what they considered their side of the Line of Actual Control (LAC) in the Chip Chap River valley, Galwan River valley, and Pangong Lake areas. On November 20, 1962, China declared a unilateral cease-fire and withdrawal to 20 kilometers behind what it described as the LAC as of November 7, 1959. During the course of the conflict, 1,383 Indian soldiers were killed, 1,047 wounded, 1,696 missing, and 3,968 taken prisoner; Chinese losses were 722 killed and 1,697 wounded. Only two Indian divisions had been in the theater when the conflict broke out, facing at least five Chinese divisions. In Namkachu, one Indian battalion faced three Chinese regiments alone, with predictably disastrous results.

THE INDIA-CHINA BORDER

The India-China border was largely unpatrolled and left to its own devices by both sides for several years after the 1962 conflict. The Chinese were preoccupied with guerrilla activity in Tibet, the Cultural Revolution, and the arduous job of building their logistics in Tibet. They withdrew in 1962 to 20 kilometers behind the so-called LAC of November 7, 1959, which they described only in general terms on maps not to scale. It was verbally described by China as corresponding, by and large, to the McMahon Line in the east (with the exception of Khinzemane) and to the Chinese boundary claim line in the western sector. In his November 1959 letter to Prime Minister Jawaharlal Nehru, Premier Zhou Enlai said that the LAC was "the so-called McMahon Line in the east and the line up to which each side exercises actual control in the west."[5]

In both 1959 and 1962 India had rejected the concept of a Line of Actual Control, arguing that the Chinese concept was a disconnected series of points on a map that could be joined up in many ways; the line should omit gains from aggression in 1962 and therefore should be based on the actual position on September 8, 1962, before the Chinese attack; and the vagueness of the Chinese definition left it open for China to continue its creeping attempt to change facts on the ground by military force. As Nehru said during the 1962 war, "There is no sense or meaning in the Chinese offer to withdraw twenty kilometres from what they call 'line of actual control.' What is this 'line of control'? Is this the line they have created by aggression since the beginning of September? Advancing forty or sixty kilometres by blatant military aggression and offering to withdraw twenty kilometres provided both sides do this is a deceptive device which can fool nobody."[6]

Zhou's written response was that the LAC was "basically still the line of actual control as existed between the Chinese and Indian sides on 7 November 1959: To put it concretely, in the eastern sector it coincides in the main with the so-called McMahon Line, and in the western and middle sectors it coincides in the main with the traditional customary line which has consistently been pointed out by China."[7]

The Chinese declaration of a cease-fire and withdrawal to 20 kilometers behind what China called the November 7, 1959, LAC after the 1962 conflict was unilateral and not dependent on Indian acceptance. It was probably caused as much by logistical difficulties in maintaining PLA troops in their forward positions in territory taken from India during the war and the Himalayan winter approaching as by the limited military and strategic value of the territory in most places. Equally, the LAC that China said it would respect in 1962 coincided with the boundary settlement that Zhou had proposed to Nehru in 1960. This created a presumption that China was willing to settle the boundary on the basis of the status quo that emerged from the war. Even if that was true then, it is certainly no longer true today.

In actual fact, in the eastern sector the LAC (whether of November 7, 1959, or September 8, 1962) for the most part coincided with the high Himalayan watershed—the basis of the McMahon Line—in India's view, the international boundary in this sector. The exceptions were significant in a local tactical sense in Longju and Asaphila, Arunachal Pradesh, and strategically significant where the line joined the Bhutanese boundary near Thagla and Sumdorongchu. In the western sector as well, there were differences in areas such as Sub-Sector North, and in Depsang, Demchok, and Chushul, between what the Chinese claimed was the LAC, which they professed to respect, and what India considered the actual position on the ground on September 8, 1962, on the eve of the Chinese attack. India was in no position for several years to actually assert a presence up to either the LAC or what India believed to be the international boundary. Soon after the war, each side unilaterally declared that it would not attempt to alter the status quo on the border by force, and China pledged to respect its version of the LAC.

After 1962, as India's capabilities improved with time, the country began to conduct air and satellite surveys, limited reconnaissance became possible on foot, and some military presence began to be reestablished by the mid-1970s. The Chinese had in the meantime used their easier access on the Tibetan Plateau to greatly improve their infrastructure, and by the mid-1970s the PLA no longer stayed 20 kilometers behind the Chinese version of the LAC in all places. The Chinese hold on Tibet had strengthened after Nixon's visit in 1972 had led to the CIA cutting off assistance to the Tibetan rebels, and by the end of 1974 the last remnants of the Tibetan guerrillas, the Chushi Gangdruk, had been chased by the PLA and Nepalese army through Mustang and the adjacent Himalayas and eliminated as an effective fighting force.[8]

In 1976, on the basis of the much better information regarding the border available to India, the Cabinet Committee for Political Affairs established the China Study Group under the foreign secretary to recommend revised patrolling limits, rules of engagement, and the pattern of Indian presence along the border with China. Throughout this period each side slowly moved up to the line, asserting presence through periodic patrols in an intricate pattern that crisscrossed in areas where both states had different interpretations of where the LAC was.

Inevitably, by the mid-1980s Indian and Chinese patrols were coming into more frequent contact with each other, ultimately ending up in a face-to-face confrontation, this time in the Sumdorongchu valley, which the Chinese called Wangdong, east of the tri-junction with Bhutan and close to the location of the initial spark leading to the 1962 conflict. In May 1986 India's annual patrol of the area, which had begun in 1983, discovered that the PLA had occupied the Indian patrol point. The Chinese had chosen their ground carefully. McMahon's original map, based on limited knowledge, showed Sumdorongchu north of the line that he had drawn on the map, even though it was south of the high watershed, the principle his line claimed to follow. Indeed, McMahon had drawn his line with a thick nib in red ink, which covered a 5-kilometer swath of territory in some places. When India formally protested the Chinese presence in Sumdorongchu in July 1986 to Chinese vice foreign minister Liu Shuqing, he responded with a straight face that, just as India had done, China was improving border management and that the PLA would no longer be bound by its self-imposed limitation of staying 20 kilometers behind the LAC.

What followed in Wangdong (Sumdorongchu) is well known. India moved in troops, occupied the dominating Longrola and Hathungla heights, and set up posts meters away from those of the Chinese. It took seven years of negotiation to stabilize the situation and, broadly speaking, to restore the status quo in Sumdorongchu. The standoff, however, served a political purpose. During Rajiv Gandhi's visit to Beijing in December 1988, India and China agreed to negotiate a boundary settlement, and that pending that settlement they would maintain peace and tranquility along the border and explore ways of keeping the peace. The two nations also agreed they would not let the absence of a boundary settlement prevent them from developing relations in other spheres.

BOUNDARY SETTLEMENT

If the evolving ground situation provided reasons to explore ways to legally ensure peace on the border with China by mid-1992, it was also apparent that boundary negotiations, which seemed likely to progress as a result of Rajiv Gandhi's visit to China in December 1988, were stalled.

China's position on a settlement progressively hardened, reflecting either the leadership's limited ability to change settled policy or the sensitivity of the territorial issue in a rising tide of nationalism, making difficult the give-and-take required for a settlement, even if it were just to convert the status quo into a boundary.

While visiting Delhi in 1960, Premier Zhou had suggested that China might recognize the McMahon Line boundary in the east in return for India accepting the Chinese claim line in the west, in effect moving the boundary from the Kunlun to the Karakoram watershed in the west, which would give China strategic depth along the Aksai Chin road between Xinjiang and Tibet (now China National Highway 219) and fix the status quo. The last time China explicitly raised this solution, though its proposal was not fleshed out, was in Deng Xiaoping's 1982 conversation with Gopalaswami Parthasarathi, the ambassador to China just before the 1962 conflict and a confidante of then prime minister Indira Gandhi. This Chinese proposal was not raised again during the multiple rounds of official talks on the boundary question from 1981 to Rajiv Gandhi's visit to China in December 1988. Instead, Chinese officials began saying in the 1980s that Beijing would compromise only if India made major adjustments first, adding that once India indicated concessions in the east, China would indicate its concessions in the west. In 1985, China specified that the concession it was seeking in the east was Tawang, in Arunachal Pradesh, something that any government of India would find difficult to accept, as this was a settled area that had sent representatives to every Indian Parliament since 1950. The Indian Supreme Court had also held in the Berubari case in 1956 that the government could not cede sovereign territory to another government without a constitutional amendment, though it could make adjustments and rectifications in the boundaries of India. The official Indian map when the constitution of India came into force in 1950, incidentally, had shown the entire western sector with a color wash and the annotation "boundary undefined," but had shown the McMahon Line boundary as a settled international boundary in the east.

Rajiv Gandhi therefore used much of his December 1988 conversations with China's supreme leader Deng and Premier Li Peng to explain that no Indian government could make significant territorial concessions, particularly in the east, and that only adjustments would be possible.[9] Though discussions on the boundary during the visit were inconclusive, Gandhi's keenness to settle the boundary was evident. He stressed his intention to do so after the general elections of 1989. (He lost those elections and was assassinated by the LTTE, the Liberation Tigers of Tamil Eelam, before he could return to government and have a chance to implement his ideas.) Gandhi's visit raised the level of talks on a boundary settlement. A Joint Working Group headed by the foreign secretary and his Chinese counterpart was set up, but its discussions in 1989 and thereafter continued in the old rut of the previous official talks and made no progress toward a boundary settlement. In the aftermath of the killings in Tiananmen Square in June 1989 it seemed unlikely that a beleaguered Chinese leadership would be able to break with past positions to settle the issue. Nor were the short-lived governments in Delhi from 1989 to 1991 in any position to address the boundary issue meaningfully.

THE INTERNATIONAL CONTEXT WAS also changing rapidly, and the old certainties were no longer valid for either India or China. For China, the unipolar moment, when the United States was the sole remaining superpower, after the collapse of the Soviet Union in 1989, coincided with the display of U.S. military might and technology in the First Gulf War of 1990 and with the revelation of deep fissures within the Chinese leadership, culminating in the Tiananmen Square killings in 1989. I was living in Beijing in 1989 and had seen posters in the square during Gorbachev's May visit asking, "Where is China's Gorbachev?" It could well be that Deng's disquiet at what he saw in the Soviet experiments with glasnost and perestroika made him more ready to use force to crush the democracy movement in Tiananmen Square in 1989. After the Soviet Union collapsed, the Chinese leadership, at Deng's prodding, studied the causes of Soviet failure. They concluded that the significant causes were Soviet overreach in attempting an arms race with the United States, the weakness of the Communist Party and its leadership, and the internal economic fragility of the Soviet Union. It appeared to the Chinese leadership, and to Deng in particular, that for China to avoid these traps—at a time when the American political scientist Francis Fukuyama was declaring the end of history and the beginning of a new, liberal, free market world order— would require time and considerable effort. China, therefore, had to avoid provocation, had to give its enemies in the United States no excuse or chance to achieve regime change in China as they had in the Soviet Union and other eastern European countries. This approach was summed up in Deng Xiaoping's Twenty-Four-Character strategy of 1992: "Observe calmly; secure our position; cope with affairs calmly; hide our capacities and bide our time; be good at maintaining a low profile; and never claim leadership."

For India as well, the collapse of the Soviet Union made old foreign policy certainties invalid. Politically, India had to come to terms with the new U.S.-led world order. India had followed a nonaligned policy since Prime Minister Nehru's time, not joining either bloc or alliance in a world divided between the United States and the Soviet Union. But in the early 1990s it was hard to be nonaligned when there was no one to be aligned with or nonaligned against. Moreover, India had begun an ambitious attempt to open up and liberalize its own economy in 1991, and that also required an extended period of peace in which to recover from the Indian economic collapse and crisis of 1990–91 and to set the country on a new trajectory.

It was clearly time for something different in India-China relations. The international context, the evolving situation on the ground along the border, and the lack of progress in settling the boundary required change. It seemed logical that in these circumstances, it would serve both Chinese and Indian purposes to try to impose peace along the border while leaving to the future the more politically difficult task of settling the boundary.

The question for India was on what basis, apart from the status quo, could peace be maintained? No basis other than the LAC suggested itself. The status quo was the LAC, irrespective of what had been said about it in the past. But accepting the legal validity of the LAC represented a major shift in India's stand. It took considerable persuasion to convince purists in the Ministry of External Affairs of this. Strangely, younger officials were less willing to contemplate this change in attitude toward the LAC. The iron had entered their souls, and they were less aware of the infirmities and ambiguities in the formal positions of each side. After internal discussion in 1992, Foreign Secretary Dixit and Prime Minister Narasimha Rao agreed that India would draft an agreement whereby both sides would commit not to change the status quo or use force, and to respect the LAC, without prejudice as to their respective stands on where the boundary lay. The reference to the LAC would be unqualified, making it clear that it was the LAC at the time the agreement was signed that would be respected, and not some notional idea of where it was in 1959 or 1962. (This had the unintended side effect of further incentivizing the forward creep to the line by both militaries, which had already led to the face-off in Wangdong.)

It was apparent that there were differences between China and India about where the LAC lay in some areas. Face-offs or confrontations had occurred in at least thirteen places where patrolling limits overlapped. India therefore inserted a provision that both sides would mutually agree on and clarify the LAC wherever necessary in the draft of the agreement.

This provision became one of the hardest parts of the agreement to negotiate. To begin with, the Chinese insisted they would respect the LAC of November 7, 1959, and that if there were any doubts, they would tell the Indians where the LAC lay. This arrogation was patently one-sided and unfair. Chinese Foreign Office mandarins seemed hard-pressed to justify this position to us, finally saying privately that they had no leeway as the PLA were insistent. The final solution was to accept the need for clarification in the 1993 agreement and much more explicitly in its follow-up, the November 29, 1996, Agreement on Military Confidence-Building Measures. The 1993 agreement created an expert group of diplomatic and military personnel to "advise on the resolution of differences between the two sides on the alignment of the line of actual control."

Apart from this aspect, the rest of the negotiation went smoothly and quickly, the Chinese accepting most of the Indian draft in toto. By June 1993 we had an agreed text initialed by the negotiators, and the agreement was signed during Prime Minister Narasimha Rao's visit to China on September 7, 1993, in Beijing. Known formally as the Agreement on the Maintenance of Peace and Tranquility along the Line of Actual Control in the India-China Border Areas, its shorthand name is the Border Peace and Tranquility Agreement.

The September 7 agreement was the first of any kind relating specifically to the border between the Republic of India and the People's Republic of China. It broke new ground in many ways. It formalized in an international treaty a bilateral commitment by India and China to maintain the status quo on the border. In effect, the two countries promised not to seek to impose or enforce their versions of the boundary except at the negotiating table. This was a big decision for India, where public sentiment was still aggrieved by the defeat of 1962, when the Indian Parliament had passed a resolution demanding that every inch of Indian territory be recovered from Chinese occupation. If it were not for Prime Minister Rao's cold calculation of national interest and his ability to quietly persuade his political allies and opponents, the agreement to maintain the status quo would have been a bridge too far, as it was initially for some of my colleagues in the Ministry of External Affairs.

The September 7 agreement effectively delinked settlement of the boundary from the rest of the relationship, and delinked it also from the maintenance of peace on the border. Both countries also formally renounced the use of force to settle the issue.

The agreement spoke of military confidence-building measures to be mutually agreed to in the future, including restrictions on air activity and limits on the size of military exercises near the LAC, and the possible redeployment of forces. This last was of great interest to the Chinese. We explained that the terrain on both sides was different, access on the Indian side was much harder, and therefore, there could be no mathematical equivalence. The two sides finally agreed that confidence-building measures should be based on the concept of "mutual and equal security" rather than on parity or other simple formulas. The restrictions on air activity and military exercises were soon worked into separate agreements, and over the next decade (and more), China and India agreed on a series of detailed agreements, mechanisms, and even standard operating procedures. The much more detailed listing of military confidence-building measures in the 1996 Agreement on Military Confidence-Building Measures[10] was a direct offshoot of the 1993 Border Peace and Tranquility Agreement, as have been other measures the two governments subsequently agreed on to keep the peace along the border. These agreements have been respected and implemented by both sides, in the main, and exceptions have been corrected quickly.

But two portions of the Border Peace and Tranquility Agreement have yet to be implemented or discussed in detail by the two countries. One is the provision that "military forces in areas along the line of actual control will be kept to the minimum level compatible with the friendly and good neighbourly relations between the two countries." The other is the provision for "mutual and equal security," which has not yet been discussed conceptually or explored or implemented by China and India, even though it provides a theoretical basis for mutual and reciprocal security, which could prove valuable as technology, trade and travel, and new military capabilities and an increased military presence on both sides of the border make accidents and mistakes more likely.

Did the 1993 Border Peace and Tranquility Agreement serve its purpose? It certainly has in terms of keeping the peace and the status quo for almost a quarter century, and in terms of the various arrangements that have made the India-China border one of the most peaceful ones India has. Of course, this is not only because of the agreement itself but also because the overall political and other interests that led to the Border Peace and Tranquility Agreement being negotiated have continued to operate. At a time of financial and economic stress and transition for the Indian economy, India managed to keep defense expenditures around 2.4–2.8 percent of GDP through the 1990s and into the first decade of the twenty-first century.[11] The agreement was only one factor, if a major one, making this possible; others included the decision to become an overt nuclear weapon state in 1998. But the point is that the agreement served—and was seen by others as serving—India's strategic interest in peace.

The Border Peace and Tranquility Agreement made legally binding reality both governments' stated determination to move beyond the 1962 conflict. This was easier for China, for it was the victor in that conflict, while India still bears psychological scars from 1962. (Mao was wrong when he told the Politburo in October 1962 that the effects of the war would last only thirty years, a short period in the long history of Sino-Indian friendship, in which only one and a half wars had ever been fought.[12]) With the Border Peace and Tranquility Agreement the two states signaled that daily state-to-state relations had been delinked from the restrictions and inhibitions of the war, and underscored their determination to keep the peace rather than to seek retribution or revenge on the border. It thus permitted the expansion of bilateral relations in other areas, despite the boundary question remaining unsettled.

Today India and China are more engaged with each other than ever before. Bilateral trade expanded sixty-seven times between 1998 and 2012, and China is India's largest trading partner in goods. (For goods and services together, the United States is the largest trading partner for India.) We have seen joint India-China military exercises in 2007, 2008, and 2013. And there are more than 11,000 Indian students in China.

As a result of the train of events set off by the 1993 agreement, the India-China border is very different from India's international boundary and Line of Control with Pakistan. With Pakistan, India has for the most part an agreed-upon international boundary. For the rest, the Line of Control, delineated on a map signed by the directors general of military operations of the armies of India and Pakistan, has the force and international sanctity of a legal agreement behind it. Nevertheless, both the international border and the Line of Control with Pakistan are "hot" or "live," crossed by terrorists and militants, and regular cross-border firing occurs. With China, the LAC is a concept; neither the LAC nor the boundary is agreed upon by the two countries, let alone delineated on a map or demarcated on the ground. Yet this is probably India's most peaceful border in the last thirty years, with no terrorists or cross-border firing. The last death on the border was in October 1975 at Tulungla, and that was by accident. The fundamental difference is that India faces a military situation on its borders with Pakistan that has been created by the Pakistan Army, whereas with China it faces a very different kind of political and strategic challenge.

Since the LAC is the basis of the peace, and peace would remain fragile without an agreement as to where the line lay, when negotiating the agreement Indian diplomats pressed for both sides to together clarify the entire LAC. Initially the Chinese agreed to clarify it only where there were differences, but subsequently they agreed to a procedure to exchange maps of where each country thought the LAC lay. This was done for the middle sector, then for the LAC in the western sector. In retrospect, this procedure gave both sides an incentive to exaggerate their claims of where the LAC lay. Once the Chinese saw the Indian map of the western sector, they balked at continuing. They argued that fixing the LAC in this manner would make it the boundary even though both sides, for different reasons, did not accept the status quo as the basis of a settlement. The process of LAC clarification has effectively stalled since 2002. India therefore does not have an agreed-upon delineation of the LAC with China. (To speak of a 10-kilometer or a 50-kilometer intrusion in these so-called disputed areas, as some journalists and officials do, is therefore not strictly accurate.)

In practice, however, the lack of clarity has not prevented both countries from keeping the peace, for three reasons. First, each side has a fairly good idea from the other side's patrolling patterns and other behavior of where the other side thinks the LAC lies. Second, both sides have, by and large, kept to their interpretation of the LAC, avoided provocation, and implemented the operating procedures and other confidence-building measures that the agreement called for. And third, both sides have not been in direct contact along most of the line. Even in the areas that both consider as lying on their side of the line, the sixteen or so areas of different perceptions of the LAC or contested areas, both sides have generally refrained from establishing a permanent presence or changing the status quo significantly.

What India has successfully done with China since Rajiv Gandhi's 1988 visit and under successive governments of different political complexions has been to maintain the peace while strengthening itself, seeking partners in the extended neighborhood and among major powers, and engaging China. Finding the balance between rivalry and incentives for good behavior, between competition and cooperation, is among the hardest tasks in strategy.

That the effort has been successful so far, despite the far more assertive Chinese policy on China's periphery since 2008, was shown by the Depsang incident of May 2013. Unlike the Sumdorongchu incident, when the Chinese set up a post on the Indian side of the LAC in 1986, in 2013 India discovered the new Chinese presence on its side of the line immediately, took countermeasures and moved in force within days, and insisted that the status quo be restored before it would discuss any of the matters the Chinese tried to raise. In 1986 this resulted in a seven-year standoff, which was only partially defused on the ground. On the other hand, in Depsang in 2013, India succeeded in getting the Chinese to vacate the area within three weeks.

To a great extent this was because of India's improved capabilities, which left the Chinese in no doubt that India could embarrass them. It was also because of the mechanisms and standard operating procedures that India and China had put in place since the Border Peace and Tranquility Agreement of 1993. The international context helped as well, though it was never explicitly mentioned. The Chinese were aware of political support for India coming from several significant countries. I mention this in some detail because it is important that the Indian strategic community draw the right lessons from our experiences. The key to arriving at a successful outcome was keeping public rhetoric calm and steady, displaying strength, and giving the adversary a way out, which was our preferred solution. It was not tweeting or whining in public, brandishing our nuclear weapons, or threatening war, as some Indian television channels and commentators did during those three weeks in May 2013.

A SITUATION IN FLUX

The situation described above appears to be changing. Since the global financial crisis of 2008–09, China no longer seems to be following Deng's Twenty-Four-Character strategy. China's behavior in the South China Sea and East China Sea has been much more assertive. On the India-China border the picture is not so stark, but here too Chinese behavior is changing.

China improved its border infrastructure significantly in the 1980s and 1990s, while India has done so in the past decade, strengthening infrastructure and positions all along the border with China. India has done more in the past ten years to strengthen and build border infrastructure and military preparedness and to create offsetting and asymmetric capabilities than in any decade since independence. These efforts have included the first new military raisings since the 1970s of two mountain divisions and now a mountain strike corps on the India-China border; reoperationalizing advanced landing grounds (airfields) in Arunachal Pradesh, on the border with China; implementing the India-China Study Group's and General Staff's suggestions for roads (intended primarily for defensive purposes), begun in 2005; the creation of imaging intelligence and technical intelligence capabilities, including intelligence gathering through the deployment of drones; and the introduction of Su-30s fighter aircraft and heavy lift aircraft into the eastern sector. The C-130 landings at Daulat Beg Oldi, in the state of Jammu and Kashmir, western sector, in 2013 were visible symbols of India's determination and improved capabilities. India has strengthened and tasked its intelligence capabilities, and has a survivable deterrent in place. But India is still playing catch-up on this border.

The situation may be changing because the balance of forces on the border has been changing, and both sides are adjusting their behavior. China and India are now in much more frequent contact. India's patrolling and assertion of presence are more conspicuous than in the past. In almost all the contested areas, India's forces are more frequent visitors than the PLA. For their part, the Chinese now find it harder to achieve their political goals on the border: to maintain undisputed military dominance, to convey a clear message to civilians and military that they are the bigger and more powerful party, and to change or create facts on the ground in their favor. While India plays catch-up in the face of a large and in some respects growing infrastructure gap, the Chinese measure themselves against the situation of unchallenged dominance that they enjoyed for an extended period after 1962.

That is why in recent years China has pressed in negotiations for an agreement that would effectively freeze the present situation on the border, preventing further infrastructure development and enhanced deployments that India might undertake. Having done what it wished to in terms of building up its capabilities, China would now like to freeze the existing imbalance. Indian representatives have naturally resisted this effort and made counterproposals of their own seeking to limit China's assertive behavior, and have pressed for clarification of the LAC, which the Chinese reject.

Is there a way out of this impasse? The 1993 Border Peace and Tranquility Agreement itself spoke of the goal of "mutual and equal security" and of agreement on force levels. If both countries so choose, this language could offer a way forward to consolidate peace on the border. India's diplomats will only know whether this is possible if we test the proposition in negotiations with our Chinese counterparts.

One example of a change in Chinese behavior on the LAC came during President Xi Jinping's September 2014 visit to India: the PLA entered Chumar, one of the sixteen areas where the LAC is disputed, in larger numbers than ever before, and did not leave for well over a fortnight. This was unlikely to have been a rogue PLA action, conducted without the knowledge of Xi Jinping, chairman of the Military Affairs Commission and the National Security Council. If it was a rogue action, the prospect should worry the world. Usually, Chinese negotiating postures are prepared, signaled, and matched by behavior on the ground. Since we saw similar behavior by the PLA when it intruded in unprecedented numbers during Prime Minister Narendra Modi's April 2015 visit to China, we can rule out the idea that these were the actions of a rogue or overly enthusiastic PLA commander on the ground. In any case, no one has been sacked for these actions, so far as is known. Indeed, the local commanders have been promoted.

There are three possible explanations for the timing and nature of PLA actions during the Xi and Modi visits. The most benign explanation is that China was serious about negotiating the boundary and wanted to convince the new Indian government of the need to do so to avoid future political embarrassment. The second is that China wanted to press India to accept its proposals to freeze the present situation on the LAC as the price for continued peace on the line. If either of these were actual causes of the PLA's intrusions, they should have been followed up at the negotiating table. This does not appear to have happened. We are therefore left with the third explanation—that China wished to emphasize to the new Indian prime minister its military dominance and ability to embarrass India on the border; that it was not so preoccupied by its troubles with Japan and Vietnam in the East and South China Seas as to need to make concessions to India; and that peace on the border is fragile, and China should not be taken for granted. In other words, the third explanation is that the PLA movements were an early attempt to establish psychological dominance over a new Indian government.

What should India's strategy be in dealing with China on the LAC? India has not tried to match the PLA's strength weapon for weapon, acquisition for acquisition, or dollar for dollar. Instead, diplomatic efforts have focused on convincing China that any misadventure would result in embarrassment and pain to that country and would frustrate the leadership's political goals. This requires asymmetric actions and capabilities on the part of India. India's strategy has been to keep the peace without ceding ground, building up preparedness steadily while pushing for a settlement of the boundary as a whole.

There has been some talk of "theater switching" in Indian defense circles, of using India's strength in the Indian Ocean, should China be tempted to use its strength on the land border. The deterrence that maritime strength gives India is not directly relevant to handling the situation on the long, disputed India-China boundary, but it is certainly necessary to defending India's growing maritime interests when the Chinese are heading toward basing and other arrangements in Gwadar, Djibouti, and the Gulf and other portions of the Indian Ocean littoral.

Overall, however, India must continuously reevaluate its strategy, since the balance of power is constantly evolving. I am not the best judge of whether or not a mountain corps is the best military answer to the Chinese challenge on the line. The broader picture is that India faces an increasingly confident China with access to Russian military technology and energy, thanks to the West pushing Russia in Ukraine into Chinese arms; with an economy that even at a slower 3–5 percent rate of growth is still the second-largest and one of the fastest-growing economies in the world; and with an increasingly nationalist and chauvinist national narrative replacing the lost ideology and mock humility of the past. On present trends, even if China continues to spend only 2 percent of its GDP on defense, by the mid-2020s it will be spending as much as the United States. China today is pursuing Xi's "China dream," building a new Asian order from the bottom up in terms of the One Belt, One Road initiative, pipelines, roads, railways, fiber-optic cables, and infrastructure projects such as ports throughout the Eurasian land mass and the littoral of the Indian Ocean and western Pacific.

I have no doubt that China wishes to be number one in the world. As patriotic Chinese, convinced that China was number one in the world order until the aberration of the last two centuries, it is natural that Chinese leaders will try to take the place of the United States as world superpower. A few years ago the Chinese Communist Party got CCTV to air a series on rising powers in history. This was after the Politburo had scholars study and learn lessons from previous rising powers, some of which succeeded in becoming number one, including Britain and the United States, and some of which failed, such as Germany, Japan, and the Soviet Union. The leadership wanted its own people to know the results of those studies. The studies showed that when rising powers made the mistake of taking on the reigning hegemon and challenging the existing order too soon, they failed—as Wilhelmine Germany and 1930s Japan had failed. The Soviet Union, for instance, made the mistake of entering into an arms race with the United States that it could not win. China's strategy today, vis-à-vis the United States, is illuminating: it privileges economy, diplomacy, and force, in that order. There is much to learn from this approach.

Whether China will succeed in its quest to become number one is an open question. China is a lonely power, geographically hemmed in, in a crowded neighborhood where others are rising too, and preoccupied with internal stability and regime survival. But it has surprised the world consistently for the past thirty years and could continue to do so.

From India's point of view, it is China's silence or ambivalence about the rise of India that poses a puzzle and a challenge. While the United States has moved from opposition to India's nonalignment in the 1950s to encouraging India's rise in the twenty-first century, China has moved in the opposite direction, from professed friendship and common cause (expressed in the 1950s slogan, *"Hindi-Chini Bhai-Bhai"*—"Indians and Chinese are brothers"), to the modus vivendi between 1988 and 2008, to the present set of Chinese actions, which constrain India's pursuit of Indian interests in the neighborhood.

Indians ask why India allows China in South Asia, and why, when China has an encirclement strategy for India, does India not have an encirclement strategy for China? Both India and China are too big to be encircled. We live today in a world in which no one can claim an exclusive zone or area of influence, a globalized world where power reaches everywhere. We should not flatter ourselves that China is fixated on encircling India. The drivers of Chinese foreign policy are likely to remain the quest for status and the acquisition of power—political, military, and economic. China has a greater goal, to become the preeminent power in the world, and India as a major power is dealt with as part of that strategy. In other words, India-China relations do not fall into a simple binary opposition but exhibit a complex interplay in political, economic, security, and other realms.

The pattern of competition side by side with cooperation will likely continue to mark the relationship in the short term. One thing that could affect this prognosis is the fact that India and China (and Japan) have seen the rise to power since 2012 of conservative, authoritarian centralizers, conservative by the standards of their own parties and societies, with little experience of central government and foreign policy and strong ideological predispositions to nationalist, even chauvinist rhetoric. Though the leaders have been careful in their public utterances, the terms in which foreign and security policies are discussed in China and India (and Japan) have become much more shrill. Antiforeign views, jingoistic slogans, intolerant ideas, and downright bad manners are common, and not just on the Internet. These behaviors would not matter in normal times, but governments today are under stress, and could seek external release from internal difficulties.

Nevertheless, I am not pessimistic about the future of India-China relations. Both countries have shown the ability, after a disastrous start in the late 1950s and 1960s, to learn from experience and to reorient policy, and both have a long tradition of statecraft to draw on. Strategy consists of making the most of available means to achieve one's goals. India's goal is to transform India. China, like the United States, or the world economy, for that matter, is a fact of life. Indians must learn to use the rise of China to achieve our goals. Where it is a hindrance, deal with it—prevent it, eliminate it, work around it, divert it. That is strategy, not a listing of tanks and weapons. And if all else fails, wars are won by a combination of men, ideas, and weapons, not just one of those factors.

Avoiding war and attaining one's goals is the highest form of strategy by any tradition or book, whether the strategist is Kautilya (Chanakya), Sun Tzu, or Machiavelli. The Indian government's record over sixty-eight years of independence shows it has not done badly in moving toward the main goal of transforming India. And that requires that the national security calculus be continually adjusted to reality even as the overall goal is kept in view.

LESSONS OF THE BORDER PEACE AND
TRANQUILITY AGREEMENT

What lessons can be drawn from the experience of negotiating and implementing the Border Peace and Tranquility Agreement?

This agreement was easier to negotiate than anything else I have negotiated with China in forty-two years. Why? The fundamental goals of the negotiation were clear and agreed on from the start. Both sides knew what the problem was, solutions were expressed simply and directly in the first Indian draft, and both sides were clear on how to achieve their goals. Most important, both sides were willing to compromise long-standing positions to reach the goal of maintaining the peace.

There are lessons to be drawn about Chinese negotiating behavior, too.

It seemed very important to China that Indian negotiators accept the term "Line of Active Control" at the beginning of the negotiation. Classical scholars would call this "names being rectified" in the Confucian sense. In the classical Chinese negotiating lexicon, the ultimate goal of insisting on the acceptance of Chinese definitions and terms for a negotiation is to establish moral and psychological dominance over an adversary as a necessary corollary to the correct ordering of the negotiation. Classical Chinese texts, such as the "Comprehensive Mirror in Aid of Governance" (資治通鑑 or Zizhi Tongjian), contain several expedients to achieve these goals. For the pessimist, Sun Tzu and the Thirty-Six Stratagems provide considerable material. A specific "barbarian-handling" tool box was first described by its early practitioner, the scholar and imperial adviser Lou Jing (婁敬) in 199 BCE, and has fed foreign paranoia ever since. More academically and positively inclined foreigners believe that Chinese culture for the past 5,000 years has been based on communities, strong morality, holistic thinking, and cynicism toward foreigners. Today, Chinese negotiators are comfortable if their adversaries are in awe of China's history, statecraft, and power, or, all else failing, Chinese intellectual superiority.

The term "Line of Actual Control" was useful to China from the 1950s until the late 1980s in providing a shifting, open-ended concept of the status quo that China could use to prevent the border from becoming militarily live except where China wished it to be. By 1992 it was clear to both countries that the status quo on the border was unlikely to be changed militarily in the immediate future. Troops from both sides had moved back up to the line and were in contact at most militarily significant points. It had now become the common interest of both India and China to maintain the de facto status quo in practice. (The broader political causes for this shift were external to the negotiations and included India's economic reforms, the end of the Cold War, the collapse of the Soviet Union, the Tiananmen killings, and so on.) The LAC was therefore the basis of the commitment not to use force to alter the situation in the Border Peace and Tranquility Agreement of 1993, the first ever exclusively border-related agreement negotiated between the Republic of India and the People's Republic of China.

Did the Border Peace and Tranquility Agreement delay a boundary settlement? This point is debatable. It certainly reduced the immediate incentive to settle the boundary to keep the peace. But the fundamental reason the boundary settlement is taking so long, to my mind, is that both sides think that time is on their side, that their relative position will improve over time. Both cannot be right. But so long as both believe this, a settlement will move forward only very slowly.

An assertive China is unlikely to seek an early settlement of the boundary issue no matter how reasonable India may be, even though the technical work has all been done. Fifty years of stability on the border suggests that give-and-take on the basis of the status quo is the logical way forward. However, China's other interests, including its relationship with Pakistan, its suspicions about Tibet, and its desire to maintain levers in its relationship with India, suggest that a boundary settlement is not a Chinese priority at present. Add to this China's dependence on the Indian Ocean and its suspicions about India-U.S. defense cooperation and strategic coordination, and forward motion seems unlikely.

Taken together, these factors make it likely that China will keep the boundary issue alive as a lever in its relationship with India. Nor would a leadership that increasingly relies on nationalism for its legitimacy find it easy to make the compromises necessary for a boundary settlement. (This is equally true of India.) That is one reason why public Chinese rhetoric on the boundary has become harsher in the last few years, and why China has increased its demands for Tawang, which no Indian government could concede, even as the Chinese military posture on the border has not changed. In other words, settling the boundary, though technically possible, is politically unlikely.

But there is more to India and China than the boundary. In fact, the overall salience of the boundary in the relationship has diminished considerably over time, now that the Border Peace and Tranquility Agreement of 1993 and subsequent confidence-building measures have stabilized the status quo, which neither side has tried to change fundamentally in the last thirty years, even as each side has improved its own infrastructure, capabilities, and position.

Bilaterally, China is now India's largest trading partner in goods, while India competes for global markets. Today, more than 11,000 Indian students study in China, and mechanisms are in place to deal with issues such as transborder rivers and the trade deficit. And on several global issues in multilateral forums both countries have worked together, each in pursuit of its own interests—the WTO, climate change negotiations, and so on. So even if India and China do not settle the boundary, there is much to be done and addressed bilaterally and by working together on the world stage.

I am convinced that we are in a moment of opportunity for India-China relations as a result of the rapid development of both countries in the last thirty years, of what we have achieved bilaterally in this period, and of the evolution of the international situation. I would go so far as to say that each country could benefit its core interests by working with the other. But to realize that potential, it is essential that both countries understand each other and the reality and perceptions that guide each other's actions.

Are there broader lessons to be drawn about India's foreign policy from this experience?

Thirty years after a traumatic defeat in war, India was willing to put the past behind it and move on, pragmatically accepting reality for larger reasons of state. The government of India was willing to change its stand on the LAC in return for the freedom to concentrate on other internal and external priorities, the most important of which was the stabilization and reinvigoration of the Indian economy through opening up and liberalization.

This shift, given the emotional baggage carried by the relationship with China and the trauma of 1962, was only possible because of some hard work and clever politics outside the public gaze at Prime Minister P. V. Narasimha Rao's behest. When we began negotiating the Border Peace and Tranquility Agreement in July 1992, Prime Minister Rao asked me to regularly brief former policymakers and opposition leaders, including Gopalaswami Parthasarathi, Kocheril Raman Narayanan, Inder Kumar Gujral, A. B. Vajpayee, and others. Each of them was a potential opponent of what we were proposing. At the very least, they would ask, "How can you trust the Chinese?" I pointed this out to Prime Minister Rao and said I really had no answer for them, not even, at that point, having an agreement or a negotiating text. The prime minister said, with a half smile, "Go and tell them what you want to do and ask them what they think you should do. Then go and do what we have agreed. And keep seeing them every two months or so." During these conversations, I learned a great deal and got ideas for the negotiation. Interestingly, it was not the China experts, such as Narayanan or Parthasarathi, who gave me the most ideas. It was A. B. Vajpayee, invariably supportive, who suggested a political way forward by asking me whether the idea of equal security for both India and China could be reflected in the agreement. This was essential for the Indian people, he said, after the trauma of the 1962 conflict. The result was the principle of equal and mutual security, reflected in the agreement and in subsequent confidence-building measures. Whenever I brought a fresh suggestion or idea to him, his first question always was, "Do you think this is good for India?"

With Prime Minister A. B. Vajpayee, one always got the feeling that he thought of a greater good than immediate party political advantage, and that he had a larger sense of India's destiny and of the historic nature of what we were doing. He was good enough to send me to China as ambassador in 2000 when our countries' relations were in cold storage after India's 1998 nuclear tests, and to Pakistan as high commissioner when we resumed relations at that level in 2003 after the 2001 attack on the Indian Parliament (by jehadi terrorists with Pakistani ISI support), and the military buildup on the border. In both cases Vajpayee's instructions were simple and clear: "You are responsible for changing this relationship. Tell me what we can do, and do what you consider is right."

As a result of the conversations with political leaders, when the Border Peace and Tranquility Agreement was announced in India on September 7, 1993, initially there was deafening silence, and then voices in support of the agreement came from across the political spectrum. There seemed to be more disquiet in the ranks of Congress and in the prime minister's own party about abandoning Nehru's legacy. But the main elements of the agreement—abjuring the use of force to settle the boundary, and respecting the status quo—had been declared in Parliament by Nehru himself in the dark days after the 1962 war.

It became clear that opinion in the country had moved on. While a boundary settlement giving up our territory was still a highly sensitive issue, no one wanted another live border when Pakistan was doing its best to foster terrorism in Jammu and Kashmir state and militancy there was at its height. And Prime Minister Narasimha Rao had shown wisdom by leading public opinion while building consensus and bringing along his political opponents as well.

CHAPTER TWO

Natural Partners

The Civil Nuclear Initiative
with the United States

Diplomats do not combine means with a view to ends, like engineers;
they take risks, like gamblers.
> —RAYMOND ARON, *Peace and War:*
> *A Theory of International Relations*

Men and nations behave wisely once they have exhausted all other
alternatives.
> —ABBA EBAN

THE ANNOUNCEMENT OF THE India-U.S. Civil Nuclear Initiative by
Prime Minister Manmohan Singh and President George W. Bush in
Washington, D.C., on July 18, 2005, was met with stunned incredulity
in India and much of the world. The agreement represented a direct attack on the most intractable problem that had bedeviled the relationship
for more than thirty years. It was the Indian peaceful nuclear explosion
of May 1974 that had led to U.S. sanctions against India, to the nuclear
controls and restrictions in the Nuclear Suppliers Group (NSG) and before it the Zangger Committee (Nuclear Exporters Committee),[1] and to
the U.S. Nuclear Non-Proliferation Act of 1978, which tightened the
terms of U.S. nuclear cooperation with other states, privileging other
nuclear weapon states (NWS) and insisting on safeguards on all nuclear
material in other states. The U.S. ambassador to India, Harry Barnes,
had even threatened India's prime minister Indira Gandhi, saying "We

will make a horrible example of you" when he heard there might be another Indian nuclear test in the early 1980s. For thirty years India had been subject to U.S. and international nuclear and technology sanctions. That India was still making progress in nuclear and space technology and was moving toward becoming a player in this arena internationally had only strengthened the voices of those in India who thought that anything worthwhile in the Indian economy had to be done autonomously and indigenously, and further, that the world would only deal with India as an equal once the country had developed its capacities on its own.

And yet here were the Indian and U.S. governments agreeing to amend their laws and to work together to strengthen the international nonproliferation regime. Seven years after India tested nuclear weapons and declared itself an NWS, India and the United States were ready to get the same NSG to permit civil nuclear commerce with India once India had separated its nuclear weapons program from its civilian uses of nuclear energy, had placed a certain number of civilian reactors under International Atomic Energy Agency (IAEA) safeguards, and had taken other steps to bring its own laws in line with the international nonproliferation regime. The United States abandoned its demand that India, as a non-nuclear weapon state (NNWS) in U.S. law and under the Nuclear Non-Proliferation Treaty,[2] accept safeguards on all its nuclear facilities, thus making a unique exception for India. In effect, India was now to be treated like the other NWS for the purposes of civilian nuclear commerce.

Both sides recognized that India had an exemplary nonproliferation record, having consistently resisted temptation. Unlike Pakistan, India had not sold or given nuclear and missile technology to others, even though it had developed the entire fuel cycle on its own and was legally free to engage in such sales. And nothing that India had done to build its own nuclear program or to test nuclear weapons flouted international law or India's commitments to others or its obligations under international law.

Once it was clear that India's nuclear weapons were off the table, India, afflicted by an energy crisis, tired of "outlaw" status, and now publicly recognizing its interest as an NWS in the existing order and in preventing the emergence of more NWS, was ready to work with the United States. In return for cooperation on civil nuclear energy programs, India was willing to subject international supplies and some of its civilian program to IAEA safeguards. India was ready to work with the

United States to strengthen the nonproliferation regime, working toward a Fissile Material Cut-off Treaty[3] and joining export control regimes. These steps represented a considerable realignment by India in return for the prospect of cooperating with the world in peaceful uses of nuclear energy.

These were big and unprecedented choices for the Indian establishment. On the eve of the planned July 18, 2005, announcement, Prime Minister Manmohan Singh's closest advisers were split on whether to proceed. Thirty years of U.S. efforts to cap, freeze, and roll back India's nuclear program had scarred the country's atomic scientists, engineers, and diplomats. Some of the prime minister's advisers argued that there was no certainty that subsequent U.S. administrations would take the same approach as President George W. Bush. Why align with a power that had been an unreliable partner in the past on an issue as crucial as India's energy future? There were other available options: India could have chosen not to do anything in the nuclear area, or to concentrate on building other, less difficult aspects of the relationship; these choices would have been much easier. The argument in the prime minister's suite in Blair House between the initiative's proponents and opponents was so intense that Prime Minister Singh decided to tell the Americans he would not go ahead with the announcement. It was only after further meetings with his team, and with Secretary of State Condoleezza Rice on the morning of July 18, and after renewed U.S. assurances, that Singh reconsidered and decided to make the announcement. This became the July 18 Joint Statement.

The two governments understood that the path to implementing this understanding was not going to be easy. It would require a series of complicated steps: amending the U.S. Atomic Energy Act of 1954, which prohibited civilian nuclear trade with nonsignatories to the Nuclear Non-Proliferation Treaty; negotiating a bilateral Section 123 Agreement, specified by the U.S. Atomic Energy Act of 1954, laying out how the two governments would implement cooperation;[4] India negotiating an India-specific safeguards agreement with the IAEA and its approval by the IAEA Board of Governors; the NSG agreeing by consensus to make an exception to permit civil nuclear trade with India; and finally, the U.S. Congress (with a House controlled by the Republican president's opponents, the Democrats) approving these agreements and arrangements. In the event, despite doubts and opposition, it took only three and a half years for all these politically and technically complex steps to be accomplished. By December 2008, political heavy lifting on both sides had made it possible for all the intergovernmental steps laid out in July 2005 to be completed before President Bush left office in January 2009.

There could have been no more potent symbol of Prime Minister Manmohan Singh's and President Bush's determination to forge a new India-U.S. strategic partnership. The larger ramifications of what was proposed were immediately clear to friend and foe alike. Opposition was quick to manifest itself, from traditional nonproliferation ayatollahs in U.S. think tanks and elsewhere, from those in India who saw cooperation on civil nuclear trade as an alliance with the United States, and from powers such as China, which saw their comfortable assumptions about India's foreign policies shaken. Russia, which was already building nuclear power reactors at Kudankulam in India, was quick to catch the wave and cooperate with India, but China began a form of diplomatic guerrilla warfare against the initiative. In India, however, the initiative quickly caught the imagination of the young, aspirational generation that was emerging. In the long months of internal politics that followed, every poll consistently showed strong popular support, and this, buttressed by the determination of Prime Minister Singh, sustained the Civil Nuclear Initiative in India.

Both India and the United States were ready for the leap that the initiative represented. The Indian imperatives were clear. The indigenous nuclear program was running out of domestic uranium to sustain the ambitious power targets that 8–10 percent annual GDP growth required. The United States was an essential partner if India was to achieve its developmental goals of building a modern, prosperous nation and eliminating poverty. And the evolution of the international system, particularly the rise of China, made it essential that India and the United States build on their strategic congruence.

The international context and the ambitious goals of the first Manmohan Singh government, outlined by him immediately after coming to power in his May 2004 interview with Jonathan Power, required a high level of understanding with the sole superpower, the United States. If India was to carry forward to its logical conclusion the peace process begun by the Vajpayee government with Pakistan, if it was to vigorously seek a boundary settlement with China,[5] and if it was to ensure a peaceful external environment in order to concentrate on using the supportive international economic environment for rapid growth and fundamental transformation, the United States would be critical to the endeavor. In each case the United States could be either spoiler or enabler for India to achieve its goals. Prime Minister Atal Bihari Vajpayee had earlier recognized this and had begun the process of transforming the relationship with the United States, referring to that nation as a "natural ally" and working closely with the Clinton and Bush administrations. The Civil Nuclear Initiative promised and symbolized a much closer relationship with a more supportive United States, with which there was now strategic congruence in several areas. The events of 9/11 had brought declared U.S. policy much more in line with long-standing Indian views on terrorism. In Afghanistan, U.S. opposition to the Taliban and al Qaeda coincided with India's approach; and on a range of bilateral issues, including defense, the U.S. administration under President George W. Bush was much more solicitous of Indian interests and concerns than previous presidential administrations had been.

The United States had come to the initiative from a conviction that there was a strategic need to build a better partnership with India. As early as the 2000 presidential campaign, Condoleezza Rice had argued in an article in *Foreign Affairs* foreshadowing the Bush foreign policy that the United States

> should pay closer attention to India's role in the regional balance. There is a strong tendency conceptually to connect India with Pakistan and to think only of Kashmir or the nuclear competition between the two states. But India is an element in China's calculation, and it should be in America's, too. India is not a great power yet, but it has the potential to emerge as one.[6]

The 2002 National Security Strategy, drafted by U.S. State Department counselor Philip Zelikow, said that "differences remain including India's nuclear and missile programs and the pace of India's economic reforms. But while in the past these concerns may have dominated our thinking about India, today we start with a view of India as a growing world power with which we have common strategic interests. Through a growing partnership with India we can best address any differences and shape a dynamic future."[7]

From the Indian point of view, these expressions of U.S. interest in India's rise would have been meaningless had the United States been prepared to build nuclear reactors in China, as it had, but not in India. While unspoken by both partners, China's rise was a factor that had created contiguous interests for both India and the United States.

Indeed, both governments had worked to transform India-U.S. relations over several years and administrations. They had laid a political basis for this change since the collapse of the Soviet Union and the subsequent realignment of great power relations. External Affairs Minister Jaswant Singh's fourteen rounds of talks on managing the effects of the Indian atomic weapons tests of May 1998 with Deputy Secretary of State Strobe Talbott between June 1998 and July 2000, though inconclusive, had made it clear that rollback was no longer feasible and that dealing with India as a de facto NWS was probably the best option. The U.S. reaction to Pakistan's May–July 1999 adventure in Kargil, the March 2000 visit by President Clinton, and the common ground against terrorism after the 9/11 terrorist attacks on the United States all helped build the political confidence to address an issue as thorny as India-U.S. nuclear differences. Strategic congruence and confidence had also been built by the successful experience of naval cooperation after the Indian Ocean tsunami in December 2004.

Though both sides had differing stakes in the relationship, the mutual political commitment to see it through was evident from the fact that the United States was agreeing to exceptions in India's favor just when it was also negotiating a tightening of terms and conditions on the Iranian and North Korean nuclear programs, to prevent those states from doing precisely what India had done: test a nuclear weapon and declare themselves NWS. The difference was that unlike India, Iran and North Korea were both in material breach of their solemn legal commitments, having signed the Nuclear Non-Proliferation Treaty as NNWS, while India had never signed the treaty or closed off its legal option to become an NWS. Nor had India ever concealed what it was doing.

The initial result of work by India's center-right National Democratic Alliance (NDA) government and the Bush first-term administration was the January 2004 Next Steps in Strategic Partnership (NSSP) initiative, which represented incremental gains in defense and technology exchanges, including the possibility of some cooperation in nuclear and space technology. The NSSP initiative also provided for discussions on ballistic missile defense, and contained India's commitment to align its export control regime with the NSG's guidelines and Missile Technology Control Regime stipulations.[8] In May 2005 India passed a comprehensive Weapons of Mass Destruction (Prohibition) Act to prevent the export of technologies and material that could be used for such purposes.[9] The Indian export control lists were also shared with the United States in advance of Prime Minister Singh's July 2005 visit to the United States.

In March 2005, Condoleezza Rice visited Delhi on one of her first visits abroad as U.S. secretary of state. She agreed with Prime Minister Singh on the need for a breakthrough in the relationship, and suggested exploring the possibility of resuming civil nuclear cooperation. India's Foreign Secretary Shyam Saran and U.S. Under Secretary for Political Affairs Nick Burns were nominated to find language for Singh's July visit to Washington. There were last-minute hitches during the visit, with the issue hanging in the balance as a result of divided counsel on the Indian side, but these problems were overcome when Prime Minister Singh decided to take the plunge.

At every stage of development of the Civil Nuclear Initiative, from its initiation by a small group of people to the negotiation of the 123 Agreement that gave it international legal form, through the legislative processes in India and the United States, the safeguards agreement and other arrangements with the IAEA, and finally the NSG clearance itself on September 6, 2008, difficult, pioneering choices had to be made by both sides. That the two nations did so consistently and successfully is testament to their faith in the strategic potential of the relationship and their ability to innovate in areas where it was not generally considered possible. An account of some of those choices follows.

UNDERSTANDING THE CHOICES

In India, one of the first questions put to Foreign Secretary Shyam Saran when he returned from Washington in April and May 2005 with ideas on how to move the initiative forward was, why should India trust the United States, a country that had reneged on its commitment to supply fuel to the U.S.-built Tarapur power reactors for their lifetime? The United States had cited domestic law, the 1978 U.S. Nuclear Non-Proliferation Act, when stopping fuel supplies to Tarapur. But that 1978 law was subsequent to the 1963 bilateral agreement that committed the United States to delivering those supplies and was a response to the Indian nuclear test of 1974, which even the United States admitted was not illegal. In India, it therefore seemed natural to ask what prevented the United States from changing its mind again. Could we rely on the United States in the future?

The real answer was that U.S. commercial, strategic, and other interests, once enmeshed in the Indian program, would ensure continuity. But
more was required to ensure this tight connection legally in the civil nuclear cooperation agreements. The solution was to agree on a set of measures, none of which violated U.S. legal provisions requiring the United
States to suspend supplies if India exploded a device. India was to be
helped to establish a "strategic stockpile" of material or fuel, and other
countries, including Russia and France, agreed to step in should there
be a break in supply. In other words, Indian and U.S. negotiators worked
around the situation that had led to the Tarapur impasse in the late 1970s
and early 1980s.

The next crisis arose when President Bush was about to visit India in
March 2006. Until that time, U.S. law envisioned only NWS choosing
which of their facilities they placed under safeguards. NNWS had to
place all their facilities under safeguards under U.S. law. For India, it
was essential that the nation's strategic facilities remain outside safeguards,
for the practical reason that the same unsafeguarded facilities, such as
breeder reactors, reprocessing plants, and fuel fabrication plants, served
both civilian and strategic purposes. India was willing to bring most of
its civilian facilities under safeguards but wished to determine for itself
which ones would come under safeguards, and when.

The issue of the number of reactors that would be in the strategic category and the number that would be voluntarily selected by India had
been resolved in advance of Bush's visit in March 2006. What remained
unresolved was the matter of fuel supply assurances and follow-up bilateral safeguards. India's position was that it would accept only international safeguards, not U.S. safeguards, and that these safeguards should
remain in place only as long as fuel supplies were assured. There could
not be permanent safeguards, and certainly not bilateral U.S. safeguards,
if for any reason supplies were interrupted. These issues could not be resolved even after hours of last-minute negotiations between National
Security Adviser Steve Hadley and Under Secretary Nick Burns, on
the U.S. side, and National Security Adviser M. K. Narayanan and Foreign Secretary Shyam Saran, on the Indian side. Anil Kakodkar, chairman of India's Atomic Energy Commission, and the prime minister's
principal scientific adviser, Dr. Rajagopala Chidambaram, were also
available for consultation. What became the paragraph on fuel supply
assurances was considered as a possible option during these negotiations,
but there were some difficult residual issues that were finally resolved the
next morning, when the principals were already meeting. (The U.S. side

had also agreed to put in a formulation on India joining the NSG, but after the sometimes tough exchanges leading to the Separation Plan, this was dropped in the course of the negotiations.)

Whether or not fast breeder reactors would be considered civilian was also contentious. India's Department of Atomic Energy (DAE) had consistently included them in the civilian category but argued that they represented "proprietary technologies" and hence could not be safeguarded.

These seemed insuperable obstacles to the negotiators until President Bush himself intervened to force a U.S. decision allowing India to decide for itself what should fall under a safeguards agreement. India argued that it was for India to decide what was civilian and what was not. In any case, should foreign-origin fuel supplies enter the fast breeder reactors after reprocessing, they would automatically fall under safeguards. This logic helped both sides overcome the impasse.

On March 2, 2006, India announced a plan to separate its civilian facilities from those for the strategic weapons program. India announced it would place fourteen of its twenty-two reactors (fifteen existing and seven under construction) under IAEA safeguards in phases until 2014. (Six were already under IAEA safeguards and eight more were to be brought in.) In fact, this was actually done ahead of the planned schedule. The United States agreed that India, like other NWS, would keep some civilian facilities such as breeder reactors out of safeguards. For India it was important that the initiative not constrain its weapons program and that India be seen to be treated as an NWS in practice.

On July 26, 2006, the Democratic Party–controlled U.S. House of Representatives approved a bill to exempt India from certain provisions of the U.S. Atomic Energy Act of 1954 by a 359–68 bipartisan vote. From India's point of view, some of the bill's provisions and some of the statements made in the debate could be seen as changing the terms of the initiative announced in July 2005. (At one stage then senator Barack Obama had mooted a killer amendment as well.) There was, therefore, considerable uproar in India. Indian opponents of the initiative accused the U.S. and Indian governments of breaking their word. Prime Minister Singh addressed these Indian concerns in his reply to a debate in Parliament on August 13, 2006, where he laid out the desiderata and the red lines that would not be crossed by India when negotiating the nuclear cooperation agreement with the United States. These included full civil nuclear cooperation; reciprocity; no internal U.S. certification requirements binding on India; India to be treated as a state possessing advanced nuclear technology (code for an NWS); an IAEA safeguards agreement and international fuel assurances; integrity of the strategic program; and no externally imposed moratorium on the production of fissile material, only a unilateral voluntary moratorium on testing.

On November 16 the Senate approved the Henry J. Hyde U.S.-India Peaceful Atomic Energy Cooperation Act by an 85–12 vote. President Bush signed the act into law on December 8, 2006. The legal mandates for the negotiators of the 123 Agreement were now clear in the form of the Hyde Act for Nick Burns, and the prime minister's solemn assurances to Parliament for the Indian negotiators. Most experts, including some of the negotiators, thought it would not be possible to reconcile the two.

NEGOTIATING THE SECTION 123 AGREEMENT

We began seriously negotiating the text of the 123 Agreement from December 2006 on. Under Secretary Nick Burns came to Delhi once the Hyde Act had given the Bush administration the legal mandate to discuss the next steps with Shyam Saran, who by now was the prime minister's special envoy for the nuclear initiative, and myself as foreign secretary. The issues were clear to both sides. The initial Indian draft, which we took to Washington in February 2007, was quite different from what the United States was used to, and the gap seemed to confirm the fears of doubters on both sides.

Resolving Differences

The three main difficulties in the negotiation related to assured fuel supplies for the lifetime of the supplied reactors, the termination of cooperation if India tested again, and the scope of cooperation (including cooperation on sensitive technologies, such as those for reprocessing and enrichment).

ASSURED FUEL SUPPLY

The United States and India had actually been among the world's first partners in the civil uses of nuclear energy. The United States had built two boiling-water reactors in Tarapur in 1963 and had committed to supply fuel for the anticipated life of the reactors. The supply ceased after the 1974 tests, in what India considered a breach of the agreement. Both sides finally arranged alternative supplies from France and Russia. The United States did so to prevent setting a precedent of a country abrogating safeguards, which India was entitled to do by the terms of the 1963 agreements with the United States and the IAEA. But the resulting bitterness was lasting, as was the psychological wound of the U.S. sanctions against India.

As a result, the first thing India sought in the 2006 initiative was the assurance of a fuel supply for the life of the plants that would be built with international cooperation. This assurance was finally provided by allowing the stockpiling of fuel by India and the promise of alternative supplies by France, Russia, and others.

Testing and Termination

For its part, the United States wanted assurances that India would not test a nuclear device again, in return for the international community agreeing to supply India with civil nuclear technology, equipment, and fuel. The U.S. president is authorized but not obligated by the U.S. Atomic Energy Act of 1954 to suspend or terminate commercial nuclear trade with any country that tests a nuclear device.

For India, this was politically a highly sensitive issue. Anything that smacked of India's being treated differently from the other NWS, particularly China, and any restriction on what the overwhelming majority of Indians think is essential for India's security with nuclear-armed neighbors, such as China and Pakistan, would invite strong reactions at home and doom the initiative. While the previous NDA government in India had unilaterally declared a moratorium on testing, the new Congress Party–led center-left United Progressive Alliance (UPA) government could not be seen to be giving up the right or the option to test under foreign pressure, especially after the previous government had resisted that same pressure in the form of the draft Comprehensive Test Ban Treaty just a few years before.

In effect, the final text of the 123 Agreement does not affect the United States' legal and statutory right to suspend civilian nuclear commerce if India explodes a nuclear device, while India retains its right to test should it choose to do so. But the agreement includes general assurances of a secure fuel supply, expresses support for India building a "strategic reserve" of nuclear fuel, and contains a U.S. commitment to see that other nuclear suppliers step into the breach if need be to ensure India's fuel supply.

Scope of Cooperation: Reprocessing
and Enrichment Technology

Reprocessing and enrichment proved much harder to negotiate. The United States adopted a tough stance on the reprocessing issue despite having conceded "full civil nuclear cooperation" in the July 18, 2005, Joint Statement. It was understood early on in the negotiations that reprocessing could not be excluded. It was on this basis that the July 18, 2005, Joint Statement included a formulation relating to enrichment and reprocessing.[10] How could India and the United States work together to stop the spread of enrichment and reprocessing technology if India was at the same time a target of the same U.S. policies and legislation?

The July 18, 2005, Joint Statement had said that "as a responsible state with advanced technology, India should acquire the same benefits and advantages as other such states." For India this was a commitment to ensure Indian access to technologies and equipment for the entire fuel cycle, including sensitive technologies such as reprocessing and enrichment. U.S. law, however, prohibited the supply of these sensitive technologies to an NNWS, and this proscription became one of the hardest issues to solve. In India this was regarded as a test of whether the United States had negotiated in good faith. The final solution, which required conversations between Prime Minister Manmohan Singh and President Bush and between External Affairs Minister Pranab Mukherjee and U.S. Secretary of State Condoleezza Rice, was for India to set up separate reprocessing and enrichment facilities under safeguards exclusively for these purposes, and for India and the United States to agree on the terms of the safeguards and other details beforehand, so that the United States could sign off on the arrangement and India could preserve its right to reprocess and enrich supplied material. The agreement to have a dedicated reprocessing facility for foreign-origin fuel was what India conceded in order to get a permanent entitlement to reprocess U.S.-origin fuel.

The Safeguards Arrangements

The negotiation of the IAEA safeguards agreement could not have been smoother. Once the principle of a separation between the civilian and weapons programs was agreed to, India had no reason to quibble about the intrusive nature of safeguards on reactors that might be built as a result of international cooperation. If anything, it was in the Indian interest that these safeguards be as thorough as possible, giving the greatest possible assurance that India was not using supplied material or equipment in its weapons program. India had nothing to hide in this part of the program. The negotiations concerning the Additional Protocol to the safeguards agreement and the India-specific safeguards agreement were smooth and quick, as mental inclinations and habits adjusted to the new reality.

Once the United States had agreed to make a significant exception for India from the insistence in U.S. law that all civilian nuclear facilities in states other than the NWS recognized by the Nuclear Non-Proliferation Treaty be under safeguards, the actual negotiation of the safeguards clauses was relatively easy. The United States chose to do this as an exemption for India rather than as a rule change in the NSG because using an exemption avoided opening the door to Pakistan and ducked the question of Israel, which denied that it had a nuclear weapon but acted on the assumption and knowledge that it did. India was quite happy to accept the most stringent safeguards since it was in the nation's interest to prove it was not diverting supplied material to weapons. (India had no need to divert materials, having its own complete fuel cycle.) India therefore also rapidly negotiated and agreed to the Additional Protocol, similar to that signed by other NWS, in just two meetings. (By 2005, fewer than one-third of signatories to the Nuclear Non-Proliferation Treaty had also signed the 1997 IAEA Additional Protocol.)[11] Difficulties arose when the United States tried to apply its templates from agreements with other countries, asking for separate flagging of U.S.-origin material and for a provision for fallback U.S. safeguards to be implemented if the IAEA was unable to implement safeguards for some reason. These difficulties were resolved by providing for material accounting while respecting Indian sovereignty.

Reactions to the 123 Agreement

Once Indian and U.S. negotiators had agreed on the text of the 123 Agreement and announced that fact on July 27, 2008, we began the process of briefing political parties, opinion makers, and others in India. We stressed that the agreed-upon text met all the criteria that Prime Minister Singh had described to Parliament on August 13, 2006: it contributed to India's energy security, promised a clean and cheap source of renewable energy, helped our nuclear program overcome the shortage of domestic uranium, buttressed our international role and position, and was a significant step in strengthening the strategic partnership with the United States.

The initial reaction from the editors with whom we spoke and even from political parties, both allies and opponents of the UPA, who came to the prime minister's Race Course Road office to be briefed, was surprisingly positive. The Communist Party of India (Marxist) delegation actually congratulated the negotiators on their achievement. I was sent to Sonia Gandhi, UPA chairperson and leader of the ruling coalition, to tell her the details. She heard me out patiently, asked the right questions, congratulated us on obtaining a good agreement, and then added that sadly, most people would look for the black spot in the dal, as the Hindi proverb has it, trying to find fault with a good thing. She was prescient. Each of the major parties ended the first briefings by saying they would have to consider what we had said with their party colleagues.

It soon became apparent that some UPA allies and a few dissatisfied Indian National Congress Party leaders saw this as a negotiating opportunity to obtain what they wanted from their own party. The opposition saw it as a useful stick with which to beat the Congress Party. They accused it of being pro–United States, of having sold out the national nuclear program, and of being anti-Muslim, because the deal supposedly implied support for the United States in its unpopular war in Iraq.

What followed was almost a year of high-level domestic political posturing and drama. The opposition Bharatiya Janata Party (BJP) opposed the initiative even though it was a direct descendant, considerably improved, of proposals their government had made to the United States in 2003–04. The Left parties, whose support in Parliament from outside the coalition was essential to the UPA government's survival, began an almost yearlong negotiation with a committee, the Group of Ministers, led by External Affairs Minister Pranab Mukherjee. Showing infinite patience and mastery of detail, Mukherjee never allowed the talks to break down, even though the Left parties were determined to scuttle the deal, or at least to drag out the process in the hope of ensuring that it never reached fruition or entered into legal force. They calculated that if they could delay the 123 Agreement's approval long enough, the next U.S. administration would not be as interested in the initiative as the Bush administration. While the Group of Ministers negotiated with the Left parties, we negotiated the text of the India-specific safeguards agreement with the IAEA and prepared to obtain the IAEA board and NSG clearances we would need. Special Envoy Shyam Saran crisscrossed the globe trying to muster the consensus we needed in the NSG and IAEA Board, and all our traditional diplomatic skills were engaged.

On July 6, 2008, the Left ran out of patience and withdrew its support for the government. A vote of no confidence was scheduled in the Lok Sabha for July 22. As soon as the vote was scheduled, we booked flights to Vienna for the night of the twenty-second. We had to brief and persuade IAEA board members on the agreements they would soon be asked to approve. The UPA government won the confidence vote late that evening with support from regional parties, including the Samajwadi Party and the Bahujan Samaj Party, and we were in a race against time to complete the remaining international steps in the initiative before the Bush administration left office in January 2009. In what must be one of the most intensive diplomatic efforts ever mounted by the government of India, we sent special envoys to each of the forty-six members of the NSG and all thirty-four members of the IAEA Board of Governors, arriving at individual understandings where necessary and working with the United States wherever possible to achieve the required consensus.

The other aspect of the July 18, 2005, understandings was that India would bring its export controls into line with the international regimes. In May 2005 the Indian Parliament had passed a comprehensive WMD Act to control the export of sensitive and dual-use equipment and technologies, and the system to enforce it was strengthened. By the middle of 2007 India could declare adherence in practice and law, though not membership, with the standards of the NSG, the Missile Technology Control Regime, the Wassenaar Arrangement (which limits conventional weapon exports), and the Australia Group (which regulates trade in dual-use chemicals). In 2008 the U.S. president was able to certify to Congress India's adherence to the NSG and the Missile Technology Control Regime and its compliance with other international nonproliferation norms.

In the course of the negotiations, the United States also raised the issue of civil liability for nuclear damage in Indian law. After examining the question in the DAE and in the Legal and Treaties Division of the Ministry of External Affairs, we came to the conclusion that it was in India's interest to adhere to the highest international legal standards if there was to be a manyfold expansion in our international civil nuclear commerce. The Vienna Convention on Civil Liability for Nuclear Damage of 1963 sets the possible limit of the operator's liability at not less than 300 million special drawing rights (SDRs) (then roughly equivalent to U.S. $400 million). Its 1997 Convention on Supplementary Compensation for

Nuclear Damages defines additional amounts to be provided through contributions by states parties. The Supplementary Convention is an instrument to which all states may adhere, regardless of whether they are parties to any existing nuclear liability convention. (Incidentally, the convention had yet to come into force.) We therefore signed the Convention on Supplementary Compensation, and proceeded to draft our domestic legislation to give that convention effect, laying down procedures for no-fault liability of the operator of a plant that has an accident.

Two aspects of the Indian Civil Liability for Nuclear Damage Act of 2010 subsequently became controversial in India and between India and the United States. One point of contention was the provision in Section 17 that the operator had a right of recourse against suppliers if their supplies caused an accident. This is not an automatic right, but such an open-ended risk worried both Indian and foreign suppliers. This problem has largely been addressed by limiting the right of recourse by amount, time, and the value of the part involved, and by contractual provisions. In addition, suppliers can now insure themselves against such claims.

The broader issue, however, was the provision in Section 46 that notwithstanding the 2010 act, no other rights under Indian law were derogated, thus opening up suppliers to tort and other claims in multiple courts, civil and criminal. This section is actually a restatement of a well-known principle of Indian and all common law systems and was operative even in the past when suppliers had worked with the nuclear program. Its inclusion in the act was politically unavoidable after the Bhopal gas accident and the Deepwater Horizon oil spill in the Gulf of Mexico, which occurred as the act was being drafted. Within a year of passage of the act, the Fukushima nuclear accident took place, adding to public concerns. If anything, criticism of the bill in India was that it sought to cap or limit the operator's liability. During and after President Obama's second visit to India in January 2015, the Indian and U.S. governments made clear their limited interpretations of this particular section. It is now up to the companies to determine whether or not this represents an acceptable risk of doing business with the Indian atomic energy program.

Obtaining NSG Clearance of an Exemption for India

The hardest task, however, was to obtain NSG clearance, by consensus of its forty-six members (in 2005), for civil nuclear cooperation with India. This was essential for the promise of cooperation to become real.

In 1992, at U.S. prodding, the NSG had agreed to allow nuclear exports only to countries that agreed to full-scope safeguards on their entire nuclear programs. Very early on we agreed with the United States to seek an exemption for India rather than a change in the NSG's rules.

The NSG met to consider the proposed exemption for India in Vienna, first in August 2008 and then again in early September. It is educative to look at the behavior of individual countries in the NSG as we worked our way through the civil nuclear initiative. In most cases, domestic political considerations were the primary determinant of country choices. Commercial interests played a role, though not to the same extent. The NSG is both a commercial cartel and a political club. Even though the majority of its members do not have a nuclear industry of their own, the consensus rule gives each of them a veto on decisions. The reliability and predictability of individual countries' behavior in the NSG vary tremendously, and to a much greater extent than realist theory or rational calculation would predict. A candid description follows of how some countries behaved before and during the NSG meetings of August 21–22 and September 4–6, 2008, in Vienna.

The United States clearly had its own game plan, driven by the administration's need to carry a Democratic Congress on the 123 Agreement, and was therefore careful in dealing with attempts by others to obtain additional commitments from India on testing or banning enrichment and reprocessing transfers, and in creating continuous leverage by adding some form of regular review, thus placing India on probation. Each of these was an alteration to the basic July 18, 2005, India-U.S. understandings. The Indian strategy was to keep these limitations and qualifications and any linkage to India's future behavior separate from the exemptions—in other words, to get a "clean" exemption with no strings attached. The United States may have been tempted to work through its allies to include demands that India had resisted in the earlier, bilateral negotiations. However, once it became clear that any conditions would lead to India rejecting the result, the United States used all its influence to obtain a clean exemption. Thus the NSG, at U.S. instance, was satisfied with a public restatement by External Affairs Minister Mukherjee of India's disarmament stances—the voluntary moratorium on testing, for instance—on the morning before the NSG decision.

The real opposition came from the "mini-six," Ireland, Austria, Switzerland, New Zealand, Norway, and the Netherlands, all of whom had no interest in nuclear trade and smaller stakes in relations with India.

They treated the NSG as a stage on which to play out their chosen roles. They postured and dissimulated in their conversations with the Indian delegation and were clearly unreliable. At the end of the process these small states with large egos chose to avoid U.S. wrath by going along with the U.S.-shaped consensus decision—one more instance of their saying one thing and doing another, pushing disarmament for others while basing their own security on the cover provided by U.S. nuclear weapons and NATO.

Brazil, Argentina, and South Africa were all helpful. Whatever their private regrets about not following India's path to NWS status, they were pragmatic and supportive when it mattered. They each had their own points of view on the issues. All three had enrichment technology and for several years had resisted U.S. efforts to secure an NSG ban on enrichment and reprocessing transfers. They were pragmatic and sufficiently integrated into the international system to work for reasonable solutions and to seek to avoid damaging their relations with either India or the United States. South Africa had a particular sensitivity about Israel, the earlier apartheid regime having worked closely with Israel's clandestine weapons program in the 1960s and 1970s, and hence was allergic to broader formulations on NSG links with "non-member adherents" in the exception for India.

Russia was well disposed but played a smaller role, being kept out of the three-power group that the United States formed with France and the United Kingdom to steer the meeting. While Russia's power to move the international system may be limited or blocked by the West, it still has a massive capacity to disrupt it. Russia's relations with the United States had worsened considerably after the conflicts in Kosovo and Georgia, but the strength of Russia's ties with India, and the fact that Russia was already building a nuclear power station at Kudankulam in India, outweighed these negative factors.

Australia, Canada, and Japan, loyal allies of the United States, each delivered in their own way. Commercial interests resulted in Canada proposing that the exemption, and therefore actual cooperation with India, only begin after 2010. This would give Canada time to conclude its bilateral cooperation agreement with India and may have suited the United States by neutralizing any head start that France and Russia had as a result of the complexity of U.S. processes.

Germany was a less than convincing or decisive chair. Some resentment of what this meant for India came out in the text Germany proposed from the chair for the press release at the end of the inconclusive August meeting. This text spoke of the complexity of the issue, of the need to consider nonproliferation aspects in greater detail and to decide on NSG policy toward India, thus opening up new and varied issues for consideration and making a positive decision less likely.

China was careful to be noncommittal, urging caution on the other members but not mentioning criteria or other countries such as Pakistan, even elliptically. China made balanced statements on the need for peaceful uses of atomic energy and for nonproliferation to be respected. Its preferences became clear in its strong support for the German chair's draft of the August press release, which was ultimately stymied by Russia and South Africa, which sought and obtained approval of a neutral and minimalist release. It was clearly China's expectation until the last minute that the mini-six would dig in their heels and prevent a consensus on the exemption. When the six changed positions overnight during the September meeting, China was unwilling to be seen as the only nation opposing the proposal, and went along. On the morning of September 6, 2008, the Chinese mission in Vienna sent the Indian delegation in the hotel a written communication that China would support the draft decision as it had been worked out, in this way avoiding being the last to support India's position. Chinese foreign office officials later blamed inaccurate reporting from the Chinese ambassador in Vienna for their stance and the "misunderstanding." But the damage to China's public image in India was considerable and lasts to this day.

And finally, India itself. India's diplomats clearly had capacity issues to resolve. It took a colossal effort and considerable disruption of our normal work for us to be able to contact each of the NSG member states and to run the campaign. If India wishes to be taken seriously by the world as a power, our diplomatic machine should be able to work three or four such issues at any one time. We are not there yet and have still to put in place the means.

Indeed, the unconditional clearance by the NSG accepting India's existing nonproliferation commitments, which were expressed again on September 5 by External Affairs Minister Mukherjee, hung in the balance until the last minute. The *Financial Times* of London actually announced the failure of the NSG meeting in its first editions for the September 6–7 weekend. Mukherjee's statement of September 5 reiterated India's disarmament commitments and policy, including the voluntary moratorium on testing as a unilateral declaration. It enabled Norway and the Netherlands to agree to the exemption for India, thus breaking the opposition by the mini-six bloc. Not until 3:45 a.m. on the day of the vote were we confident that the clearance would be granted, and the formal decision was made later that day, at 11:30 a.m., on Saturday, September 6, 2008.

It is a tribute to U.S. power and persuasion that despite the misgivings and divergence in the expressed views and interests of so many NSG members, the United States obtained a clean exemption in an acceptable form from the meeting on September 6, 2008. India's red lines were respected, namely, no reference to testing, no discriminatory provisions, and no periodic review of India's behavior or the exemption, thus permitting permanent full civil nuclear cooperation—the "clean" exemption that India had sought.

With NSG approval on September 6, 2008, the July 18, 2005, Joint Statement on civil nuclear cooperation undertakings between India and the United States had been fulfilled in all major respects, except for the U.S. Congress vote on the 123 Agreement and other amendments to U.S. law. The two governments had done what they promised. What remained was practical implementation by individual departments and commercial entities. The devil, they say, is in the details, and much practical work remained to be done. But given the sort of pioneering work that India and the United States had done to make this outcome possible, and the reasons why they did so, there is no reason to believe that they will not succeed in the future, too.

CONGRUENT OBJECTIVES, PERSISTENT INDIVIDUALS

Looking back, it is evident that the civil nuclear initiative would not have reached a successful conclusion were it not for the quiet persistence of Prime Minister Manmohan Singh in India. At least twice during the tortuous domestic process in late 2007 and early 2008, Special Envoy Shyam Saran and I argued internally that if our domestic constraints made it difficult for us to go through with the initiative, it would be best to call it off by mutual consent with the Americans, thus minimizing damage to India-U.S. relations and the prestige that Prime Minister Singh and President Bush had personally attached to the effort. It was the prime minister who insisted on letting the process in India play out, and who finally forced a decision on going ahead when—and this is admittedly hearsay—he told the Congress Party leadership that he would not stay on as prime minister if the initiative were abandoned. There is a steely resolve in Manmohan Singh that is concealed by his gentle manner. The UPA government decided to force the issue in Parliament through a confidence vote in July 2008. By then, a very senior Congress Party leader later told me, the party had also come to the conclusion that an alliance with the Communists would be a liability in the general elections due to take place in May 2009, and that abandoning the informal arrangement by which they supported the government from the outside was the best political course. But it was Singh's dogged but quiet persistence that sustained the initiative at every stage and ultimately made all the difference. Personalities matter.

The Indian side was also fortunate in having a team of professionals who knew their stuff, such as Chairman of India's Atomic Energy Commission Dr. Anil Kakodkar, Foreign Secretary and then Special Envoy Shyam Saran, National Security Adviser M. K. Narayanan, and Ambassador Ronen Sen, all backstopped by the nuclear scientist Ravi B. Grover and the diplomat Subrahmanyam Jaishankar, the sources of details and ideas. Shyam Saran in particular was indefatigable and made a huge contribution to gaining the NSG clearance and exemption with his advocacy in NSG capitals. External Affairs Minister Pranab Mukherjee was a master of the domestic political and parliamentary process required to bring the initiative to fruition. It was natural that differences would exist within the Indian team as to the best way forward, and sometimes on the substance of the Indian position. After all, this was unprecedented policy terrain. It involved abandoning several habits and shibboleths of long standing. The process of internalizing change could be painful, particularly for scientists in India's DAE, whose experience since 1974 had taught them that the U.S. goal was to stop or roll back India's indigenous nuclear program. But as the process of working out the initiative went forward, internal consensus became easier to build. The same professional competence made the major players on the Indian side confident and convincing advocates, defending and arguing for the initiative in public.

Throughout the fractious domestic political process, Indian negotiators were also sustained by the confidence that the Indian public understood the logic and supported the initiative. The media parsed, chittered, and sensationalized, depending on the prevailing winds of the day. Politicians and political parties, even established ones like the BJP, chose to support or oppose the initiative depending on their attitude toward the Congress Party government rather than on the basis of the substance of the issues or their previous conduct and stances while in government. But polls in autumn 2007 showed that 93 percent of the people of India supported the initiative for what it promised in terms of better relations with the United States and energy supplies. The noise generated by the vocal minority that opposed it had effect among the chattering classes rather than the masses. Pranab Mukherjee's tortuous negotiations with the Left lasted more than a year and seemed to be going nowhere. But, step by step, they made it possible for us to negotiate the India-specific safeguards agreement with the IAEA and to prepare for the July–October 2008 sprint to the finish line. Ultimately, in managing the narrow political interests of political parties and leaders that opposed the initiative, which included doubters within the UPA, national interest prevailed over politics. But the manner in which it worked itself out was messy, proving once again what Bismarck said about the making of laws and sausages: the less known and seen, the better.

On the U.S. side, President Bush, Secretary of State Condoleezza Rice, and National Security Adviser Steven Hadley, the drivers of the initiative, coordinated an effort across the U.S. government and in the U.S. Congress to see it through no matter what the obstacles were. Philip Zelikow, counselor in the State Department, was a source of ideas and consistently saw the strategic potential of the initiative and of the relationship with India. For instance, it took last-minute work by the White House to get the necessary votes from Congressman Gary Ackerman for the House to approve the Civil Nuclear Initiative by a vote of 298 to 117, an outcome that was uncertain until the last minute. The same was true in the Senate, where it was Deputy Chief of Staff Josh Bolton who ensured the numbers, and this at a time when the U.S. and world economy were crashing around our ears and the president was trying to get the economic crisis rescue package (or TARP) done. Nick Burns and his successor as under secretary of state, Bill Burns, did the hard work of negotiating the agreements, persuading Congress, and getting the international approvals. It was impressive to see the entire U.S. government at work to achieve its goals in the NSG and elsewhere. President Bush does not get enough credit for running an effective, like-minded, and committed team in his second term, and for his clear strategic vision. He clearly saw India as a "natural ally," in Prime Minister A. B. Vajpayee's phrase, and not just in the global war on terror. In all our meetings with Bush I found him focused, clear on the issues, well prepared, and willing to listen. I can only speculate that this son of privilege, born to the blue-blooded in the U.S. establishment, went to great pains to appear ordinary, and succeeded. But the image concealed a sharp mind and a genuine ability to connect with other people, as shown by his close and productive relationships with Manmohan Singh and Brazilian president Lula, two most unlikely partners from very different ideological backgrounds. When Bush and Singh were together, they were relaxed to the point of laughing and joking with each other. On the U.S. side as well, personalities mattered.

Both leaders had followed a high-risk strategy. The initiative could well have failed at any of the complex stages it had to go through. If the initiative had failed in the Indian Parliament, in the U.S. Congress, or in the NSG or the IAEA Board of Governors, it would have set back India-U.S. relations considerably, to say nothing of the loss of personal credibility and the political damage to the two leaders themselves.

IN RETROSPECT, WAS IT worth it? Was it worth a government of India staking its future on a no-confidence vote in Parliament on this issue, something that had never been done on any foreign policy issue in India?

My answer is yes. The Civil Nuclear Initiative was always about more than a dollars-and-cents calculation or the import of reactors, or even only about a clean and cheap source of renewable energy for India's growth. All these were important, but they were not the only or even the main drivers of the process.

On September 25, 2008, President Bush hosted a small private dinner for Prime Minister Manmohan Singh in the White House for about ten persons, when the 123 Agreement was awaiting approval by the U.S. Senate. Secretary of State Rice leaned over and asked Singh when India would be ordering reactors from Westinghouse. Bush cut her off immediately and said that this was not about reactor sales but about much bigger things. Singh did not have to reply.

The initiative stemmed from a conviction that a true India-U.S. strategic partnership would serve our national interests in the changed situation. While both countries have always fought shy of saying that their partnership is to balance China, it is clear that the rise of China was one of the major spurs. Besides the initiative also recognized the reality that India was already building Russian reactors at Kudankulam (as China was doing in Chashma, Pakistan), and that it was self-defeating for the United States to continue sanctions and to count itself out of an Indian economy that had grown at over 6 percent annually for more than twenty-five years and was then averaging over 8 percent annual GDP growth.

There is a creative tension at the heart of India-U.S. relations. India clearly needs U.S. technology, markets, and support to transform itself and create the stable and peaceful environment that the country needs to grow. The United States finds a stronger and more active India useful since there is a clear strategic congruence between the two countries' goals in the Asia-Pacific. But India is also an awkward partner since its strategic interests in West Asia diverge from those of the United States, and India's present stage of development, so different from that of the United States, leads India to make economic demands that strain U.S. preferences.

The Civil Nuclear Initiative removed the detritus of the past from the bilateral relationship, opening the way for the transfer of dual-use technology and enhanced cooperation on defense. The initiative also created an opportunity for both countries to discuss, coordinate, and cooperate on several international issues: on the Indian Ocean; on South Asia; on Nepal's Maoist insurgency, the demise of the LTTE in Sri Lanka, and Bangladesh's move away from extremism; on Afghanistan; on maritime security in Southeast Asia and in counterpiracy efforts off the Horn of Africa; on climate change; on the WTO; and on Iran—where, for instance, India played a small role in carrying messages and getting British sailors freed by the Iranians. The Manmohan Singh–George W. Bush friendship also played a role in keeping Pakistan's Gen. Pervez Musharraf honest (up to a point), and limited his scope for mischief. Bilaterally, it opened the way to a rapid expansion in trade and in scientific and technological exchanges that certainly helped India's development. And it opened up sensitive cooperation in counterterrorism efforts and intelligence gathering. Today India-U.S. relations are better than they ever have been. As a game changer, the initiative served the purposes of its initiators.

Of course, Indian diplomats did underestimate some of the negative effects of our success in seeing the initiative through. The way in which the initiative was handled domestically resulted in the politicization of foreign policy. Its entanglement in domestic politics, which is an increasingly apparent feature in the last decade, is now often expressed in a lack of cross-party consensus on major foreign policy issues.

It was not only people in India who saw the initiative as marking a much closer strategic alignment between India and the United States; so did other powers. And they naturally took balancing steps. It is arguable that the initiative was a major factor in ending the relatively balanced Chinese approach between India and Pakistan from 1993 to 2006. In 1996, President Jiang Zemin of China had publicly advised Pakistan in a speech to the Pakistan National Assembly to do with India what China was doing—discuss difficult issues but not let them prevent the development of the overall relationship. But by the time of the Mumbai terrorist attack in 2008, China was unwilling, despite the killing of a Chinese person on explicit instructions from the control room in Pakistan, to condemn or to act against the attackers and their sponsors. Since then the Chinese commitment to Pakistan and the Chinese presence in Pakistan-occupied Kashmir have grown substantially, culminating in the $46 billion commitment by President Xi Jinping to the Pakistan-China Economic Corridor in 2015. The Pakistani fear in 2005 of China being lured by India's economic prospects has now been replaced by a consolidation of the Sino-Pakistan axis.

India-China relations too have seen a hardening of the Chinese position on a boundary settlement since November 2006. The Civil Nuclear Initiative can thus be said to have provoked a natural rebalancing that we were probably slow to anticipate.

Less easy to anticipate were other developments that affected the implementation of the initiative. The global economic crisis and the accident at the Fukushima Nuclear Power Station after the March 2011 tsunami in Japan also changed both public perception and the economics of nuclear power, affecting the speed with which the initiative could result in the construction of new nuclear power plants in India.

All in all, the initiative showed that India was willing to make risky choices if its strategic purposes were served but remained cautious in negotiating and implementing those choices. For the larger purpose of a strategic partnership with the United States, Manmohan Singh's government was willing to be seen in public taking a leap of faith in the Bush administration's ability to deliver changes in U.S. law and policy toward India. The Civil Nuclear Initiative was strategically bold in its design. But when it came to negotiating the 123 Agreement and other implementation agreements, and to completing the domestic political steps required, the government of India was careful and slow, taking things one step at a time and almost leaving it until too late, until the last days of a Bush administration that had every reason to be distracted by the global financial crisis. A U.S. official who had negotiated 123 Agreements with other countries told me he had never had to explain, discuss, and argue about text and language to the degree he had done with the Indians. There is a didactic negotiating style that India has made its own over the years. But both Nick Burns and Bill Burns and their Indian interlocutors kept the larger strategic purpose in mind throughout, despite persnickety and finicky negotiations and domestic critics second-guessing every step. The government of India once again put into play the combination of strategic boldness and tactical caution that it deploys on most major foreign and security issues.

Today India and the United States are victims of the initiative's success. The emotional impact of the Civil Nuclear Initiative raised the level of ambition in the relationship so high that expectations on both sides have become hard to fulfill. This is not a problem that those who handled the relationship before 2005 ever had. While India's ties with the United States are better than ever and continue to expand, in public discourse the search continues for the next big thing, the next civil nuclear initiative. I have no doubt that having surprised the world once in July 2005, India and the United States can certainly do so again in the future.

CHAPTER THREE

Restraint or Riposte?

The Mumbai Attack and Cross-Border Terrorism from Pakistan

Any idiot can face a crisis. It is this day-to-day living that wears
you out.
—CLIFFORD ODETS in *The Country Girl*

This stain-covered daybreak, this night-bitten dawn,
This is not that dawn of which there was expectation. . . .
—FAIZ AHMED FAIZ, *Freedom's Dawn*, 1947

SOON AFTER 8 P.M. ON November 26, 2008, ten Pakistani terrorists, members of Lashkar-e-Taiba, came ashore in Colaba, the southern tip of the Mumbai peninsula, and began coordinated shooting and bombing attacks across south Mumbai. Over three days they killed 166 people and wounded at least 308. The casualties included 26 foreigners—Americans, Britons, Australians, Singaporeans, and Israelis. The attacks were on the Taj and Oberoi Hotels, the Leopold Cafe and Chabad House, the Chhatrapati Shivaji Railway Terminus, and other sites where foreigners, particularly Jews, were likely to be present. By the morning of November 28 all the sites had been secured except the Taj, where the last two gunmen were flushed out and killed on the morning of November 29 by the National Security Guard, the dedicated central antiterrorism force. One terrorist, Mohammed Ajmal Amir Kasab, was captured alive, and his testimony, along with intercepts, made it clear that the terrorists were Pakistanis, that they had been trained in Pakistan by the Lashkar-e-Taiba (LeT; literally, "Army of the Righteous") and the official Inter-Services Intelligence (ISI) of the Pakistan Army, and that they had been directed throughout the attack from a control room in Karachi, Pakistan, where Pakistan Army officers were present. Indian intelligence was monitoring those conversations in real time during the attack, leaving no doubt about the provenance and sponsorship of the attack.

There had been other, more deadly terrorist attacks in Mumbai before, all with links to Pakistan. Coordinated bombings on March 12, 1993, had killed 257 and injured more than 700 persons. Seven bombs that exploded in eleven minutes on Mumbai suburban trains on July 11, 2006, had killed 209 and injured more than 650 people. But nothing matched the level of organization, the sheer savagery, and the television spectacle of the commando-style attacks on November 26, 2008 (known by the shorthand "26/11" to most Indians), later described by the *New York Times* as "maybe the most well-documented terror attack anywhere."[1]

India and its counterterrorism partners, including the United States, had no doubt that the attack had come from Pakistan and that Pakistan's most powerful intelligence agency was involved in its organization, training, and financing. Over several years it had become clear to all of India's partners that the LeT was a creation of the Pakistan Army and had been designed for a covert war against India. Significantly, the LeT, unlike other Pakistani terrorist groups, had never attacked Pakistani targets.

Immediately after the November 2008 attacks, the Pakistan Army denied any involvement. Evidence in Pakistan was covered up. Journalists were prevented from visiting Kasab's village, and his family was spirited away by the ISI. The Pakistan Army also promulgated a red-herring disinformation campaign, claiming that India was preparing to attack Pakistan and that the Mumbai attack was a pretext, carried out by Indians and Bangladeshis. Pakistan massed troops on the border, probably expecting an Indian military response.

I am often asked, "Why did India not attack Pakistan after the 26/11 attack on Mumbai?" Why did India not use overt force against Pakistan for its support of terrorism? I myself pressed at that time for immediate visible retaliation of some sort, either against the LeT in Muridke, in Pakistan's Punjab province, or their camps in Pakistan-occupied Kashmir, or against the ISI, which was clearly complicit. To have done so would have been emotionally satisfying and gone some way toward erasing the shame of the incompetence that India's police and security agencies displayed in the glare of the world's television lights for three full days.

During and after the attack, a series of informal discussions and meetings in government took place that considered our responses. The then national security adviser, M. K. Narayanan, organized the review of our military and other kinetic options with the political leadership, and the military chiefs outlined their views to the prime minister. As foreign secretary, I saw my task as one of assessing the external and other implications and urged both External Affairs Minister Pranab Mukherjee and Prime Minister Manmohan Singh that we should retaliate, and be seen to retaliate, to deter further attacks, for reasons of international credibility and to assuage public sentiment. For me, Pakistan had crossed a line, and that action demanded more than a standard response. My preference was for overt action against LeT headquarters in Muridke or the LeT camps in Pakistan-occupied Kashmir and covert action against their sponsors, the ISI. Mukherjee seemed to agree with me and spoke publicly of all our options being open.[2] In these discussions we considered our options, the likely Pakistani response, and the escalation that could occur.

But on sober reflection and in hindsight, I now believe that the decision not to retaliate militarily and to concentrate on diplomatic, covert, and other means was the right one for that time and place.

This chapter takes up in a little more detail the immediate response, the advisability of military or kinetic action, and the options that were available at that moment; the larger issue of the utility of force in dealing with cross-border terrorism; and the broader context of India-Pakistan relations, the central role that cross-border terrorism has acquired in those relations, and the response of the international community.

THE CHOICE OF RESTRAINT

The simple answer to why India did not immediately attack Pakistan is that after examining the options at the highest levels of government, the decisionmakers concluded that more was to be gained from not attacking Pakistan than from attacking it.

Let's consider what might have happened had India attacked Pakistan. Most immediately, the fact of a terrorist attack from Pakistan on India with official involvement on the Pakistan side would have been obscured.

Instead, as far as the world was concerned, the incident would have become just another India-Pakistan dispute. India had some experience with this ho-hum reaction when it took Pakistani aggression by so-called tribal raiders in Kashmir in 1947 to the UN Security Council. The evidence clearly showed the involvement of the Pakistan Army in the invasion,[3] but the UN Security Council chose to play politics and to treat aggressor and victim similarly, and imposed a cease-fire. Ultimately the UN Security Council's intervention only made finding a solution, and eliminating aggression, more complicated. Faced with a dispute between two traditional rivals, the world's default response is to call for peace and to split the blame and credit 50:50 in the name of fairness or even-handedness. This was just what the Pakistan Army wanted. Its first reaction during the attack itself was to approach the United States and the United Kingdom asking that India be restrained from launching a war between two nuclear weapon states (NWS).

An Indian attack on Pakistan would have united Pakistan behind the Pakistan Army, which was in increasing domestic disrepute, disagreed on India policy with the civilian-elected government under President Asif Zardari, and was half-heartedly acting against only those terrorist groups in Pakistan that attacked it. An attack on Pakistan would also have weakened the civilian government in Pakistan, which had just been elected to power and which sought a much better relationship with India than the Pakistan Army was willing to consider. Zardari's foreign minister, Shah Mehmood Qureshi, was actually visiting Delhi on the night the attack began. The Pakistan minister of information, Sherry Rehman, who admitted publicly that Kasab was a Pakistani, soon lost her job under pressure from the army. In fact, the Pakistan Army mobilized troops and moved them to the India-Pakistan border immediately before the attack began, then cried wolf about an Indian mobilization. Once again, a war scare, and maybe even a war itself, was exactly what the Pakistan Army wanted to buttress its internal position, which had been weakened after Gen. Pervez Musharraf's last few disastrous years as president.

A limited strike on selected terrorist targets—say, the LeT headquarters in Muridke or the LeT camps in Pakistan-occupied Kashmir—would have had limited practical utility and hardly any effect on the organization, as U.S. missile strikes on al Qaeda in Khost, Afghanistan, in August 1998 in retaliation for the bombing of the U.S. embassies in Kenya and Tanzania had shown. The LeT camps were tin sheds and huts, which could be rebuilt easily. Collateral civilian damage was almost certain since the camps, and particularly the LeT buildings in Muridke, had deliberately been sited near or beside hospitals and schools. Even if there were no civilian casualties from Indian actions, casualties could nonetheless be alleged and produced by the ISI. The real problem was the official and social support that terrorist groups in Pakistan such as the LeT were receiving, and that was not likely to stop because of such a limited strike.

Official support also meant that the prospect of bringing the perpetrators of the attack in Pakistan to justice were near zero, and would be even lower once an Indian attack took place. So this consideration was really irrelevant to the decision.

And a war, even a successful war, would have imposed costs and set back the progress of the Indian economy just when the world economy in November 2008 was in an unprecedented financial crisis that seemed likely to lead to another Great Depression.

NOW LET'S CONSIDER WHAT did occur when India chose not to attack Pakistan. By not attacking Pakistan, India was free to pursue all legal and covert means to achieve its goals of bringing the perpetrators to justice, uniting the international community to force consequences on Pakistan for its behavior and to strengthen the likelihood that such an attack would not take place again. The international community could not ignore the attack and fail to respond, however half-heartedly, in the name of keeping the peace between two NWS. The UN Security Council put senior LeT members involved in the attack on sanctions lists as terrorists.

Pakistan itself did as little as it could against the perpetrators. The terrorists had been motivated and briefed personally by Hafiz Saeed, the head of LeT (which had renamed itself Jamaat-ud-Dawa) and were trained by Pakistan Army officers. The immediate Pakistani reaction to international and Indian pressure was to show Pakistani police officers locking Jamaat-ud-Dawa offices and to briefly place Hafiz Saeed under house arrest. But he was released in early June 2009 and is now treated by the Pakistani authorities and media as a respected social and political leader. David Coleman Headley, the U.S. national of Pakistani origin who, by his own account, undertook seven reconnaissance visits to Mumbai for the ISI and LeT, has given testimony to an Indian court about two previous failed attempts by the LeT that same year to attack Mumbai, and of the direct involvement of the ISI in planning the reconnaissance, choosing the targets, and training and equipping the attackers. In May 2009, we were given a report by the Pakistan Federal Investigation Agency that acknowledged that the Mumbai attack was mounted from inside Pakistan by the "defunct LeT." Despite this, after India presented Pakistan with undeniable evidence, evidence that the Indian Supreme Court found sufficiently credible to sentence Kasab to death, the Pakistanis still prevaricated, raised questions, sought clarifications, and finally arrested only seven lower-level members of the LeT. The seniormost detainee was Zaki-ur-Rehman Lakhvi, the military operations head of the LeT, but he was allowed to carry on his business from inside the jail, using a cell phone and receiving visitors. On January 9, 2015, he was even granted bail of U.S. $3,100 by a High Court. The other masterminds remain at large in Pakistan. Lists of thirty-seven people in Pakistan involved in the attack have been given to Pakistan. The LeT simply carries on its deadly business under its changed name of Jamaat-ud-Dawa. The perpetrators of the Mumbai attack have yet to face justice in Pakistan, despite serial promises, including some made by National Security Adviser Sartaj Aziz to Prime Minister Manmohan Singh in 2014, that they would be sentenced in two to three months.

We have had much greater success dealing with those connected with the attacks when they traveled outside Pakistan, and with those in Spain, Italy, and elsewhere who helped equip them with communications and other equipment. According to media reports, Sheikh Abdul Khwaja, handler of the 26/11 attack and Harkat-ul-Jihad al-Islami (HuJI) chief of operations for India, was subsequently picked up in Colombo, Sri Lanka, and brought to Hyderabad and formally arrested in January 2010. Zaibuddin Ansari (aka Abu Hamza, aka Abu Jundal) was arrested at the Delhi airport on June 25, 2012, after he was deported from Saudi Arabia. But the list of those responsible is long. India originally named thirty-seven suspects, including two Pakistan Army officers in the case, to which the names of David Headley and Rana were subsequently added.

The real success was in organizing the international community, in isolating Pakistan, and in making counterterrorism cooperation against the LeT effective. India began to get unprecedented cooperation from Saudi Arabia and the Persian Gulf countries, and China, too, began to respond to requests for information on these groups.

Equally, success could be measured in dogs that did not bark in the night, in avoiding the outcomes that would have resulted from a decision to attack Pakistani targets and the high probability of war ensuing from such a decision.

Internally, there was clearly a need to tighten laws and build institutions against terrorism. The Unlawful Activities (Prevention) Act was passed unanimously in December 2008, the National Investigation Agency was established, and a national counterterrorism center was proposed, which is still to be created. Other steps to ensure coordinated use of intelligence and counterterrorism actions were also taken.

Interestingly, the attack united India as no other event except a war had done. Sensing this, the political parties did not make the attack and India's response an issue in the general election campaign that followed within a few months, and the center-left United Progressive Alliance (UPA) government was voted back into power in May 2009.

All the same, should another such attack be mounted from Pakistan, with or without visible support from the ISI or the Pakistan Army, it would be virtually impossible for any government of India to make the same choice again. Pakistan's prevarications in bringing the perpetrators to justice and its continued use of terrorism as an instrument of state policy after 26/11 have ensured this. In fact, I personally consider some public retribution and a military response inevitable. The circumstances of November 2008 no longer exist and are unlikely to be replicated in the future.

The international response to our restraint was heartening in terms of the levels of cooperation in dealing with the incident. But counterterrorism cooperation is no exception to the law of international politics that each state looks after its own interests first. The United States had given us some general warnings in early 2008 that the LeT was planning to attack targets in Mumbai, but neither the scale nor the nature of the attack was clear. After the attack it became evident that several foreign intelligence agencies had pieces of the larger puzzle beforehand but had not put them together, individually or collectively, since they did not know what they were looking for. This is a common problem in intelligence, as the 9/11 experience in the United States shows.

There will also always be a suspicion in India that the United States knew much more than it admitted. The attack was prepared and reconnoitered by a U.S. citizen of Pakistani origin, David Coleman Headley (born Daood Gilani), who was a U.S. Drug Enforcement Administration agent from at least 1997 on, and who worked for both the ISI and LeT simultaneously. That the American government allowed Headley to enter a secret plea bargain and that access to him and his testimony was restricted as a result fed Indian suspicions. In fact, Headley was picked up in Chicago only in October 2009, after he had contacted Ilyas Kashmiri, the operational head of al Qaeda, in May 2009 and had begun working on targets in western Europe.[4] Headley was sentenced in 2013 by a Chicago court to thirty-five years in a U.S. prison for his role in the attacks.

After the attack the United States was conflicted between its varied interests: not allowing the Mumbai attack to stop whatever cooperation it had with the ISI in Pakistan and Afghanistan, not permitting Indian retaliation from affecting its plans in Afghanistan, and meeting the requirements of U.S. law since six Americans had been killed. The United States therefore subsequently began saying it was not sure that the higher command of the ISI and the Pakistan Army had known about the attack. India finds this demurral not credible. The director general of the ISI, Ahmed Shuja Pasha, has visited Lakhvi in a Pakistani prison. When U.S. citizens brought a suit in a New York court against Pasha, the U.S. government chose to grant him immunity. But to expect the U.S. government to behave differently would be unreasonable, in my estimation, as it has to follow its own calculus of U.S. interests rather than satisfy Indian desires.

The events of 26/11 also raised the larger question of the utility of force in responding to cross-border terrorism and nonstate actors. In India, the Israeli model is often quoted, or misquoted, in support of military action as the answer. But the Israeli model, which the Israeli political scientists Efraim Inbar and Eitan Shamir in 2013 described as "mowing the grass," is limited in aim and effect. They write:

> Israel's use of force can achieve only temporary deterrence. Therefore Israel has adopted a patient military strategy of attrition. . . .
>
> The use of force in such a conflict is not intended to attain impossible political goals, but a strategy of attrition designed primarily to debilitate the enemy capabilities . . . hoping that occasional large scale operations also have a temporary deterrent effect in order to create periods of quiet along its borders. . . .
>
> Israel's superior military power is incapable of coercing a change in their [nonstate actors] basic attitudes in the short term. . . .

> Israel recognises that it cannot affect the motivation of the non-
> state actors . . . and that producing deterrence against them is
> problematic. Yet its use of force could reduce the military capabili-
> ties of the non-state actors.[5]

The Israeli preference is for short responses against nonstate actors, not
their state sponsors, conducted primarily from the air, and for intelligence-
based operations, targeted killing, and preventive actions, such as inter-
dicting the supply of advanced weaponry to Hezbollah and Hamas.
"Mowing the grass" seeks cumulative deterrence, not absolute deterrence.
It is, like fighting crime, necessary for maintaining a minimum level of
deterrence. The use of deterrence in asymmetric warfare is questionable
unless the nonstate actors take over territory and act as governments, as
occurred with Hamas in Gaza in 2007 and with Hezbollah in Lebanon
in 2005.

There are some commonalities in what India and Israel face. Essentially, both countries face the prospect of prolonged intractable conflict
with nonstate actors. Both must deal with nonstate actors whose moti-
vation and hostility will not change with the application of military
force. In other words, deterrence is unlikely to work with them. The
American Nobel prize winner Thomas Schelling defines deterrence as
aiming to "persuade a potential enemy that he should in his own interest avoid certain courses of activity."[6] By this yardstick the LeT will
not be deterred by the controlled application of military force. While
this does not rule out punitive strikes, it does limit their utility. The
LeT shows no signs of evolving into something more benign. Realistically speaking, neither the LeT nor Hamas will evolve and join the political mainstream as the PLO or India's home-grown insurgents have
done in the past.

What the Indians and the Israelis do differs from what Western military academies teach. The West offers two basic schools of thought on
coping with nonstate armed groups (or insurgencies). The first, enemy-
centric approach suggests that such engagement is not fundamentally
different from conventional warfare, in which the main effort is to neutralize armed units by locating and engaging them. "A war is a war is a
war," as a U.S. officer once said. The second approach is population-
centric, focused on gaining the support of the civilian population, a tactic known as "winning hearts and minds," to deprive insurgents of their
main source of support. (The United States fought the war in Vietnam

as an enemy-centric war and the Afghanistan conflict as a population-centric war. Neither was a conspicuous success.)

But there are also significant differences between what Israel and India face. India confronts two types of nonstate actors: internal ones, such as the Naxalites, or members of Maoist guerrilla groups, against whom India has adopted a population-centric approach, and cross-border terrorists from Pakistan. The nonstate actors flowing out of Pakistan receive support, sanctuary, and training from a state and its army. India is not alone in having to deal with this threat. The United States and Europe also are threatened by the possibility of terrorist acts by nonstate actors that receive support from the army and the organs of the state of Pakistan. And that state and army have nuclear weapons. Further, the international environment in which India operates is very different from Israel's. These differences explain why our steps against nonstate actors and their sponsors remain covert rather than overt. If they were not, today's international environment would enable Pakistan to involve the United States and China in India's bilateral affairs and to internationalize its differences with India, as it did with the Jammu and Kashmir issue in the 1950s.

In dealing with nonstate actors and their sponsors, India uses a range of asymmetric measures designed to degrade their capabilities and to inflict pain on them and their state sponsors. We combine measures on the ground with associated diplomatic initiatives. The precise mix varies as the situation evolves. We have made advances in human intelligence and technical intelligence collection and have enhanced collaboration among India's intelligence and counterterrorism agencies to enable preventive action to be taken and to respond swiftly if incidents do occur despite our best efforts, as they inevitably will. That effort has been successful in creating periods of temporary peace along our borders.

Radical ideologies and religion cannot be defeated on the battlefield, particularly if their military manifestation has state support, as is the case with the Taliban and the LeT. (Absent state sponsorship, and in the presence of bad leadership, as in the case of the Liberation Tigers of Tamil Eelam—LTTE—in Sri Lanka, force can eliminate the terrorists' military strength, as I discuss in the next chapter.) In a conventional war, of course, we seek battlefield decision, choosing annihilation over attrition. But in the nonconventional struggle we are now engaged in we seek to subject the jihadi groups and their sponsors to unrelenting pressure—military, political, economic, and internal—none of which is in itself decisive in attaining our ultimate political objective of eliminating them as a source of threat and hostility. That is our two-step political objective, not the implausible one of changing the mind or the nature of the jihadi tanzeems (or groups) or the Pakistan Army into a benign force.

In other words, overt military force is only one weapon, and not the most decisive or even necessarily the most effective weapon, against cross-border terrorism and nonstate actors such as those that India faces. Force is indeed useful preemptively against nonstate actors. The threat of its use has some deterrent effect when the nonstate actors acquire the attributes of a state, as Hezbollah has done in Lebanon. The threat of force may also be useful in deterring the state sponsors of terrorism, such as the Pakistan Army, but even this effect is limited, as the Mumbai attack and subsequent LeT attempts prove.

These lessons also seem to apply to what is now happening in the Middle East with ISIS, and in Yemen with the Houthi rebels.

POSSIBLE MOTIVATIONS FOR THE MUMBAI ATTACK

Why did the Pakistan Army, Pakistan's ISI, and the LeT carry out the Mumbai attack when and where they did?

Several reasons suggest themselves. At every moment in the past when there was progress in the bilateral India-Pakistan dialogue, the Pakistan Army and its proxies have created an attack or diversion. The Lahore Summit between Prime Ministers Atal Bihari Vajpayee and Nawaz Sharif in 1998, which held out so much hope of a breakthrough, was followed almost immediately by Pakistani infiltration and occupation of territory on the Indian side of the Line of Control in Kargil, which provoked a short and sharp war and ended that peace process. President Pervez Musharraf's April 2005 visit to Delhi and movement toward a settlement of the Jammu and Kashmir situation on the back channel was stopped in its tracks by the June 2006 serial train explosions in Mumbai and then by Musharraf's own internal problems. In early 2008 newly elected Pakistani president Asif Ali Zardari made it clear that he wished to move forward on trade with India, said that nuclear confrontation made no sense and that Pakistan could consider no first use of its nuclear weapons, and seemed ready to pick up the threads on a Jammu and Kashmir settlement where Musharraf had left them. The Pakistan Army had opposed this initiative vehemently in Pakistan, but its internal dominance was not what it once was. The Mumbai attack put an end to an already limping peace process. It also restored the balance of power within Pakistan vis-à-vis the civilian government in favor of the army. We saw this immediately after the attack when President Zardari promised Prime Minister Manmohan Singh that he would send the director general of the ISI to India to assist in the investigations. Within hours the Pakistan Army spokesman made it clear that no such visit would take place.

The attack also solved a rift within the LeT. From 2006 to 2008, several disaffected LeT cadres left the LeT for al Qaeda in Afghanistan and global jihad. The rift was between those who wanted a more active LeT jihad in Afghanistan and Pakistan, one that would include targeting the Pakistan Army, and those who hewed to the ISI line of focusing exclusively on India. The 26/11 attack tried to settle this rift by a spectacular al Qaeda–style strike in Mumbai. It could also have been designed to move jihadi violence from the domestic soil of Pakistan to India, always an ISI goal. (The Saudis and Qataris had successfully used this tactic for years, exporting their radicals to the rest of the Middle East and Afghanistan and Pakistan.)

As with other terrorist attacks, the hope was probably that the Mumbai attack would derail India's economic progress, hence the choice of foreigners and of India's financial capital as targets. Another goal might have been to set off a communal conflagration in India, home to the world's third-largest Muslim population, over 150 million, in the hope of revenge attacks on the community. Both these calculations failed. India's period of most rapid economic growth actually coincided with the time when cross-border terrorism from Pakistan was at its most virulent in the Punjab in the 1980s, in Jammu and Kashmir in the 1980s, 1990s, and 2000s, and in the rest of the country after 1993. Deaths from terrorist violence and particularly from cross-border terrorism have declined steadily for more than ten years as India has improved its counterterrorism and intelligence-gathering capabilities and international cooperation. As for communal violence, most of the ISIS or Daesh members in custody have been brought to the authorities' attention by their own families and their own community. This does not mean there will not be deluded individuals or that incidents will not take place. But it does mean that the social cement that keeps India together is strong and significant and must be strengthened by fighting all communally divisive forces lest the fires that are raging to our west in Pakistan, Afghanistan, and West Asia find kindling in India.

Pakistan has consistently used terrorists and infiltrators against India since 1947. Pakistan has been acutely conscious of its bigger neighbor's strengths and has sought to compensate asymmetrically for its inferiority in conventional military terms—the same urge that led Pakistan to seek nuclear weapons from the early 1970s on, after the loss of Bangladesh. Pakistan sent "tribal raiders" to try to take Kashmir in 1947, infiltrators into Jammu and Kashmir in 1965, soldiers posing as mujahideen into Kargil in 1999 to occupy the heights, Khalistani terrorists into the Indian Punjab in the 1980s, and the LeT and others into Jammu and Kashmir right through this period. Pakistan's use of terrorists has been counterproductive, with results the opposite of what Pakistan intended. The tribal raiders' looting and raping in 1947 convinced the people and Maharajah of Jammu and Kashmir that their future lay with India. The infiltrators of 1965 created the war that Pakistan lost, solidifying the division of Jammu and Kashmir. The mujahideen in Kargil only got the international community, including China, to reaffirm the sanctity of the 1971 Line of Control.

India's Political Goal in Dealing with Cross-Border Terrorism

What is India's political aim in the struggle with cross-border terrorism by Pakistan and its nonstate proxies? Should India seek the Clausewitzian military goal of complete military victory, ending the conflict and annihilating its enemies? To my mind that is impractical and unreasonable. Pakistan's steady slide into incoherence, its disintegration into multiple power centers, and the diminishing writ of the state also mean that support for cross-border terrorism could actually grow in the future. Even if the Pakistani state regains some coherence, the institutional interest of the Pakistan Army and the ISI in controlled confrontation and hostility with India will enable and support terrorist groups that target India.

India's immediate political objective must recognize that this is a long conflict that cannot be solved—that it is protracted and intractable. This is an idea that most Indians are reluctant to accept and some find intolerable, but it is nonetheless gaining ground in India. Given the situation in Pakistan, the institutional interest of the Pakistan Army, and the radicalization (or Talibanization) of Pakistani society, I do not think that any other conclusion would be prudent. Knowing the limited utility of force against these groups, Indian policymakers and diplomats must be prepared for the long struggle to continue without decisive military solutions, and set ourselves modest political goals in this struggle. Temporarily silencing the cross-border terrorists is the best we can hope for. Besides, in the hierarchy of India's national goals, silencing these terrorists is of much lower priority than the transformation of India. The cross-border terrorists pose no existential threat to India. Failure in India's nation-building endeavor or prolonged economic failure would be.

Even more detrimental to Pakistan in the long run has been the effect on that country's own polity, economy, and society of its doomed quest for strategic parity with India and of its use of terrorists as instruments of state policy. Here we may consider where India and Pakistan were ten years ago in terms of security, internal development, and international standing and where they are today. This is an example of consistent policy, by different Indian governments, producing the best possible outcomes from bad situations and poor options.

OPERATIONALIZING THE LIMITED CHOICES
IN INDIA-PAKISTAN RELATIONS

It is sometimes argued in Pakistan that cross-border terrorism from Pakistan is a consequence of the state of India-Pakistan relations. "Solve Kashmir and all will be well," India is told. I am not so sure that it is any longer within Pakistan's capacity to stop terrorism now that it has so infected and become so entrenched in Pakistan's society and state.

From India's perspective, cross-border terrorism has become the major element in the relationship, the litmus test of Pakistan's sincerity. Pakistan, on the other hand, says that India should get over its obsession with Mumbai and that Pakistan has suffered as much or more from terrorism. This may be objectively true in terms of the number of casualties, but for India the issue is the Pakistani use of cross-border terrorism as an instrument of state policy, in India, Afghanistan, and elsewhere, and its segmentation of "good" and "bad" terrorists. Whether cross-border terrorism is the cause or the result of poor India-Pakistan relations is a chicken-and-egg problem that is unlikely ever to be resolved.

India-Pakistan relations are one of the few major failures of Indian foreign policy. By any benchmark this is the case. Jinnah had spoken of Pakistan being to India as Canada is to the United States. But even by less lofty standards than close alliance or a settlement of all differences, such as achieving a modus vivendi whereby each country goes its own way and leaves the other in peace, India's policies cannot be said to have achieved their goal. What has developed instead is a prolonged state of entrenched hostility with sporadic efforts to change the state of the relationship, all of which have failed so far.

The hostile state of the relationship has affected both countries, Pakistan directly by stunting its political, economic, and social development. In India's case the costs are indirect. Paradoxically, the years of the most inveterate hostility and cross-border terrorism from Pakistan are precisely the years when India achieved the most in transforming itself, accelerating economic growth and stepping out on the international stage. The costs of hostile India-Pakistan relations for India have instead been in the form of opportunities lost and roads not taken. This loss is largely counterfactual and therefore harder to prove. But could Afghanistan have developed differently were Pakistan not seeking strategic depth and trying to exclude the Indian bogeyman there? How different would Jammu and Kashmir be today had India grasped the opportunity created by Ambassador Satinder K. Lambah's back channel negotiations with General Musharraf's confidant Tariq Aziz in 2005–06 of an accord with Pakistan? Would not transit access through Pakistan have benefited India, Afghanistan, Iran, Central Asia, and Pakistan itself? These are lost opportunities that will never repeat identically, and there is no point crying over spilt milk. But certainly the state of our relationship with Pakistan has been an albatross that has hobbled Indian diplomacy and enabled other powers to gain leverage in India's and the subcontinent's affairs.

Each side has its own narrative of the causes of this failure. Indians see Pakistan as a failed state, or worse, as an integrated criminal enterprise, lacking an identity and increasingly Talibanized, perpetually seeking revenge for 1971. Pakistan sees India as hegemonist and expansionist (and therefore seeks strategic parity), says the partition of the subcontinent is unfinished—that Jammu and Kashmir should belong to Pakistan as a Muslim-majority province—and believes that India has never reconciled itself to Pakistan's existence.

There is no proof that Pakistan's responses to international pressure to cease supporting terrorists and using them as an instrument of state policy are anything other than tactical retreats and obfuscation, no matter what the costs are to Pakistan's society and polity. Pakistan still harbors the leaders of al Qaeda, the Taliban, and the Haqqani network on its territory and uses elements of these groups against India and

Afghanistan. In 2013–14 we saw hundreds of Pakistani and foreign fighters traveling to Iraq and Syria by air through Qatar and along smuggling routes through Iran to join Daesh, or the self-styled Islamic State of Iraq and the Levant, which declared its caliphate and took large swaths of territory in Iraq and Syria in June 2014.

The problem today is that the Pakistani state cannot do the things necessary to sustain the semblance of a normal relationship with India. Terrorism is hard-wired into Pakistan's society and polity, not just into the ISI. Pakistan is internally divided. No single political force, not even the army, is powerful enough to deliver outcomes, and the country is increasingly radicalized. It is hard to see this situation improving markedly any time soon. There are multiple centers of power in Pakistan, ranging from the jihadi groups and religious extremist parties, to the Pakistan Army (and its ISI), to civilian democratic politicians, businessmen, and civil society, each of them pulling in different directions and requiring a different Indian approach.

Incidentally, Pakistan is the exception to the general improvement in the situation in South Asia. In the last few years Nepal has mainstreamed the Maoist insurgents into a normal democratic party; Sri Lanka has eliminated the LTTE; and Afghanistan, though severely challenged, is more viable than it has been in the last forty years. Bangladesh has attacked the sources of terrorism and extremism in its society, and Myanmar is moving toward a normal polity. The list goes on. The security and political situation has improved everywhere on the Indian subcontinent except in Pakistan.

In light of the condition of Pakistan, it is sometimes argued that we have reached the limits of the outcomes that can be produced by normal state policy, whether of dialogue on all subjects and firmness in substance, or stopping dialogue, or other overt actions. India today lacks the power to solve its Pakistan problem, which largely stems from Pakistan's own condition. The best India can do is to manage the problem.

It did not have to be so.

In 2004–07, under Prime Minister Manmohan Singh, we came close to setting the stage for a changed relationship between these two countries, addressing Jammu and Kashmir and other issues, with overwhelming popular support on both sides of the border. That effort was stymied by domestic politics in Pakistan. In March 2007 Gen. Musharraf was in a confrontation with his Supreme Court and lawyers, and told us that he could not fight on all fronts simultaneously. He asked that we wait before taking forward the great progress that had been made through the Lambah-Aziz back channel.[7]

In July 2009, fresh from the reelection of his government, and with a new civilian government in Pakistan under President Asif Zardari and Prime Minister Gilani, Prime Minister Manmohan Singh made one more effort to pick up the threads where they had been dropped before the Mumbai attack. Meeting in Sharm El-Sheikh on the sidelines of the Fifteenth Summit of the Non-Aligned Movement, the two prime ministers agreed to resume the dialogue, to discuss terrorism, and to work for the resolution of all outstanding issues. Their joint statement to the press was immediately attacked in the Pakistan media as having conceded the Indian point that terrorism came across the border from Pakistan. On the Indian side, the opposite charge was made against the Indian government, namely, that by agreeing to discuss Balochistan, India had admitted to sponsoring terrorism there and that there should be no dialogue with Pakistan so long as cross-border terrorism took place. This criticism was illogical. If Pakistan wished to discuss its internal affairs in Balochistan with India, even if it was to accuse India of meddling, why should Indian diplomats shy away from a discussion? And it was precisely because of issues like cross-border terrorism that a dialogue with Pakistan was necessary. Every Indian government, including those led by the then opposition parties, had recognized and acted on this desideratum when in power.

I tried to make the case to our members of Parliament in a lecture soon afterward: I argued that while we might be accused of bad drafting, there was nothing wrong with the policy behind the attempt at Sharm El-Sheikh. But in the resulting media cacophony, only the first part of the sentence was picked up; my statement was portrayed as an attempt to shield the government from blame, and the policy arguments were ignored. Logic and reason stood no chance against the political self-interest and calculation of the opposition Bharatiya Janata Party (BJP) trying to deny success to a government that was the first to win reelection in twenty-five years. Even some members of the ruling party and coalition seemed to feel threatened by the media and other sections ascribing the UPA's May 2009 election victory to Singh personally. In retrospect, it may be that it was premature to resume dialogue with Pakistan nine months after the Mumbai attack. One problem was the general impression in India that while Pakistan had much to gain by way of international respectability from a dialogue, India did not. But that was a time when a new government in India and a positively inclined civilian government in Pakistan could have made a difference, if domestic politics had not intervened. To me, Sharm El-Sheikh was another opportunity squandered in the long list of missed half chances in India-Pakistan relations.

Too often in India the debate on Pakistan policy is reduced to a series of meaningless shibboleths or false opposites—to talk or not to talk, for instance. It actually makes no difference to the terrorists' behavior whether the governments talk or not, except that the advocates of not talking empower and give an effective veto to the terrorists and their sponsors over the governments pursuing the evident interest of their peoples in better relations, freer trade and travel, and the reintegration of the subcontinent's markets.

On each occasion when we had a chance to change the unsatisfactory trajectory of India-Pakistan relations—the signing of the India-Pakistan Simla Agreement in July 1972, Rajiv Gandhi's 1988 visit to Pakistan, Prime Minister Atal Behari Vajpayee's visits in 1999 and 2004, and the 2004–07 process led by Prime Minister Manmohan Singh—domestic politics, with not a little help from the great powers, has prevented us from changing that relationship. Indeed, it has complicated it further. The salience in India-Pakistan relations of the political uses of terrorism, taught and practiced in the resistance to the Soviet presence in Afghanistan, now complicates them further. As the lines are redrawn in Afghanistan and Central Asia between the United States, on the one hand, and China and Russia on the other, and as Pakistan becomes ever closer and more tied to China, India-Pakistan relations will bear the imprint and will probably pay the price.

An Indian policymaker must deal with several Pakistans—with civil society, the Pakistani business community, civilian politicians, the army and the ISI, and the religious right (which extends from political parties to jihadi tanzeems). Not all of these Pakistans have the same attitude toward India, and each responds and acts differently toward India and Indians. In effect, India is called on to run several Pakistan policies simultaneously, engaging civil society, business, and civilian politicians and containing or answering what the ISI and others attempt. This necessity exposes Indian policymakers and diplomats to accusations of inconstant policy because we are engaging in several policies and policy modes simultaneously—talking, doing business, and attempting to counter cross-border terrorism from Pakistan, all at the same time.

In the forty-odd years since the Simla Agreement was signed, in July 1972, India and Pakistan have fallen into a repetitive pattern or dance of their own. They engage in talks, the terms of which are the same, whether they are called a composite dialogue or by any other name; and during the talks some progress is achieved and small steps are taken, arousing popular enthusiasm and warmth. The moment there is a real prospect of major issues being resolved, however, there is a big disruption, most often a terrorist incident or attack, and then negotiators start the cycle all over again, first tentatively and then a little more surely. That stage of a tentative beginning seems to be where we are again in late 2015.

For this pattern to be broken, something fundamental has to change in what creates this cycle in India, in Pakistan, or in the environment. Many have tried to disrupt the cycle, and all have failed. The one who came closest was Prime Minister Singh in 2004–06. The bad news is that today, thanks to Pakistan's secular decline into irrelevance, Indian motives to address India-Pakistan issues are diminishing. The tragedy is that Pakistan is increasingly becoming a single-issue country in Indian discourse, and that issue is the zero-sum one of security. As a result, it is harder and harder to interest a young and aspirational Indian public outside the Punjab (and its colonies, such as Delhi) in the relationship with Pakistan.

THE INTERNATIONAL COMMUNITY'S MAIN interest in India-Pakistan relations today is to prevent a nuclear war from breaking out and to keep Pakistan's nuclear weapons and know-how from falling into the wrong hands.

The nuclear weapon tests of 1998 changed the interstate dimension of conflict in South Asia. They lowered the nuclear threshold and therefore diminished the likelihood of large-scale conventional war. Nuclearization did not make conventional war impossible, as the Kargil War of 1999 proved. But it did make a conventional war of the 1965 or 1971 type less likely. Even the Kargil conflict was brought about by Gen. Musharraf and his small coterie by stealth as a closely held secret within the Pakistan Army. The likelihood of international political intervention in what is now a confrontation between two NWS is also higher than it was before 1998. As Kargil showed, nuclear weapons did not prevent India fighting to recover territory, and international intervention was quick to press Pakistan to respect the Line of Control and restore the status quo. In nuclearized conditions, conventional conflict is likely to be much more limited in space and time. One thing both Pakistani and Indian establishments are agreed on is that nuclear weapons have stabilized the subcontinent.

As for the security of Pakistan's nuclear weapons, the real danger is not just from terrorists getting their hands on the weapons. (They have tried repeatedly, attacking nuclear bases throughout Pakistan.) Nuclear weapons are complex devices, difficult to manage, use, and deliver, requiring very high skill levels. Sadly, terrorists have easier and cheaper ways of wreaking havoc. To my mind the real threat is from insiders, from a Pakistani pilot or a brigadier who decides to wage nuclear jihad, with or without orders. This risk increases as Pakistan builds tactical nuclear weapons for battlefield use, control of which will necessarily be delegated down the chain of command. Pakistan's is the only nuclear weapon program in the world that is exclusively under military control. There are good reasons why no other country chose to go down this path.

TERRORISM, FORCE, AND THE LIMITS OF STATECRAFT

The attack of 26/11 led Indian policymakers to consider deeply the utility of force in dealing with terrorism and nonstate actors, and the choices available to states when faced with these situations. It seems that while force is useful, it is of limited utility in eliminating terrorism when it has state sponsorship.

In fact, terrorist acts are often designed to provoke the use of disproportionate force by the victim so as to achieve the terrorists' political ends. In this case, a decision to go to war or to strike Pakistan would have played into the LeT's and Pakistan Army's plans.

Terrorism depends for its success on the victim's cooperation, on his behaving as expected. It is the political effect, the publicity, that is the terrorist's oxygen. It is the disproportionate response to his act that the terrorist seeks to provoke. He thus selects his targets for their psychological and political impact, even if his real capacity to inflict kinetic damage is limited. What force can do is help to create the conditions for the other actions necessary to eradicate terrorism by its roots in the community. For that, force—its calculated and clever application—is a necessary condition. But it is not enough.

Are there wider lessons here, for West Asia and the fight against ISIS, for instance?

There is a school of thought that argues that it was not 9/11 but the reaction to 9/11, the so-called global war on terror and the invasion of Iraq, that made al Qaeda's rise and expansion inevitable, leading ultimately to other, more extreme splinter groups such as ISIS. If the global war on terror has been a failure it is because it did not target the epicenters of jihadi terrorism, whence terrorism derived its ideological, financial, and state support—Saudi Arabia, Qatar, Pakistan, and now Turkey. ISIS grew because of the marginalization of Sunnis in Iraq and the hijacking of the Syrian revolution by jihadists. I would add two more reasons: the consequences of upsetting the regional geopolitical balance (in Iran's favor) when Iraq was eliminated as a factor by the First Gulf War, and the political and institutional fragility of the societies where ISIS and its brethren flourish.

From what we have seen of the utility of force in dealing with such terrorism, it would seem that preemption and subsequent intelligence-based operations need to be supplemented by the hard political and social building of institutions. Without stronger institutions, bombing from the air or ground troops is seldom a sufficient answer.

A related issue is how the creation of artificial or weak states, as occurred in the entire belt from the Mediterranean Sea to the Indus after the two world wars, coincides with the area where religious extremism, separatism, and terrorism now flourish. Is there a link not just to weak state formation and capacities and governance but to externally induced partition and artificial boundaries? Sykes, Picot, and Radcliffe and the other drawers of artificial boundaries to suit imperial convenience have much to answer for.[8]

India's choices in November 2008 in response to the Mumbai attack were determined by what it saw as its own national interest at that time. That calculation was unique to that time and place and is not likely to be repeated exactly. Politics and security offer no simple formulas or methods to calculate and enhance security.

Other states too made similar calculations of national interest in their individual reactions to the event. The United States was torn between its divergent interests. Each state developed its own calculus. As a result, although low-level individuals outside Pakistan have been brought to book for the attack, its real perpetrators have not. The 26/11 attack, like the 9/11 attacks in the United States or the London subway bombings, cannot be said to have brought about systemic change in the way the international community deals with terrorism. There are more efficient means of cooperation and coordination today, and there is somewhat better sharing of intelligence among the like-minded. But the proposed Comprehensive Convention on International Terrorism, which the UN has debated for more than twenty years, is still stuck without an agreed-on definition of what is a terrorist. Over the ensuing eight years, such sanctions and limits as were placed on Pakistan after 26/11 have withered away. And it is business as usual for the LeT and Jamaat-ud-Dawa despite the Pakistan Army's fight against some sections of the Pakistan Taliban after June 2014.

The aftermath of the Mumbai attack also revealed the limits of diplomacy. Just as force has limited utility in these situations, so does diplomacy. While force is limited in its uses by objective factors, diplomacy is limited by selfish calculations of national self-interest by each sovereign nation-state—which, after all, remains the basic unit of statecraft. And by taking the fight outside what states normally do, the terrorist or non-state actor limits the use of traditional statecraft. Policymakers the world over have yet to come to terms with this shift in the world. We talk of a borderless world for humanitarian efforts and even of a right to protect, but we have yet to arrive at an international doctrine or consensus on how to prevent harm, which should precede interventions justified by a so-called right to protect. If the events of 9/11 and 26/11 did not provoke change in the international system, and so long as states are jealously protective of their sovereignty, it is hard to see the current situation improving.

Last, personalities matter. With a different mix of people at the helm, it is quite possible that India would have chosen differently. In fact, if India is forced to make a similar choice in the future, I am sure it will respond differently.

CHAPTER FOUR

Force Works

Sri Lanka Eliminates
the Tamil Tigers, 2009

Conciliation failing, force remains. Force failing, no further hope of reconciliation is left.
—EDMUND BURKE, *On Conciliation with America*, 1775

Do not feel safe. The poet remembers.
You can kill me but another is born.
The words are written down, the dead, the date.
—CZESŁAW MIŁOSZ, *Collected Poems: 1931–1987*

BY JANUARY 2009, the twenty-six-year-old civil war in Sri Lanka was clearly heading for a crisis or to resolution, depending on one's point of view. For over a year and a half the Liberation Tigers of Tamil Eelam[1] (or LTTE) had been starved of supplies by sea, thanks to effective intelligence and interdiction by the Sri Lankans and the Indian Navy, and help from other countries. And the Sri Lanka Army (SLA) had changed tactics. It had stopped trying to bring the Tigers, an essentially guerrilla force with main force features, to decisive battle. Instead the SLA was undertaking the steady grind required to clear and hold territory taken back from the LTTE in the north, using long-range reconnaissance patrols to target LTTE leaders. This was done with ruthless and patient efficiency, and with disregard for the cost in civilian and combatant lives. The writing was on the wall for the LTTE's autocratic and undisputed leader, Velupillai Prabhakaran, who had formed and led one of the most feared and deadly terrorist groups in the world.

PRELUDE TO CONFLICT

How had affairs come to this pass?

The roughly 2.2 million Sri Lankan Tamils, about 11 percent of Sri Lanka's population when the war began, had been in Sri Lanka for more than 2,000 years. Over time they had evolved very differently from the 60 million Tamils in India. They were also distinct from the so-called Indian-origin Tamils brought by the British to Sri Lanka in the nineteenth and twentieth centuries to work on coffee and tea plantations, who constitute about 4 percent of the population. The Sri Lankan Tamils, largely concentrated in the north and east of the country and in the capital city, Colombo, were a highly educated and influential minority in the country. They had taken to English education first and had benefited in terms of power and employment when the British ruled Ceylon. The Ceylon National Congress, modeled on the Indian freedom movement's political party, the Indian National Congress, was formed in 1919 to represent the entire population of Ceylon. The next year, British governor Sir William Henry Manning responded and sowed the seeds of divide and rule by introducing "communal representation," which worked to the Tamil minority's advantage until 1948.

There were multiple religious and ethnic fault lines in Sri Lanka, the former Ceylon, between the primarily Hindu and Christian Sri Lankan Tamils and the predominantly Buddhist Sinhalese, with a sprinkling of "Burghers," who had some Dutch blood; Muslims concentrated in the capital Colombo and the Northern and Eastern Provinces; and other small communities. In colonial Ceylon, the Muslims had an economic influence greater than their numbers would suggest, while the Sri Lankan Tamils dominated the professions and civil services. Many Muslims were Tamil speakers. While Tamil speakers of all religions were concentrated in the north and east, the areas claimed by the LTTE as Tamil Eelam, their homeland, the Sinhalese were concentrated in the south and west of the island.

For India, whatever happened in Sri Lanka directly affected the far larger population of Tamils in the southern Indian state of Tamilnadu, the scene of an active separatist movement with considerable popular support through the 1950s and early 1960s. In his maiden speech in the

Indian Parliament in November 1962 the leader of the largest separatist party called for the establishment of a separate "Tamil Eelam" or homeland for Tamils. Through the 1960s, however, these political groups were steadily mainstreamed into abandoning these demands, and they now constitute the ruling parties in the province of Tamilnadu, which is fully integrated into the Indian union.

Developments in Sri Lanka, however, moved in the opposite direction. With independence for Sri Lanka in 1948 came majority politics and a series of steps that disadvantaged the Tamil minority. The 1948 Ceylon Citizenship Act made 700,000 Indian-origin Tamils stateless; the 1956 Sinhala Only Act, formally the Official Language Act No. 33, replaced English with Sinhala as the only official language; in the 1970s a preferential university admissions system known as the "policy of standardization" discriminated against Tamils in recruitment to jobs and university places and institutionalized ethnic discrimination; and officially sponsored colonization in the north and east by Sinhala farmers aroused Tamil resistance. The Tamil United Liberation Front (TULF), a political party devoted to Tamil rights, took the first steps in the 1950s and 1960s to organize Tamil resentment and resistance politically. By the 1970s Tamil grievances had spawned militant groups among "our boys," as establishment Tamil politicians called them. One of them was the Tamil New Tigers, formed in 1972 by Velupillai Prabhakaran and Chetti Thanabalasingham (the latter a petty criminal from Kalviyankadu). They adopted the tiger as their symbol because the Chola Empire had done so when it ruled territory stretching into Southeast Asia from its capital in Thanjavur in India between the sixth and the thirteenth centuries. In 1976 the TULF hardened its stance to demand self-determination for Sri Lankan Tamils and the creation of a socialist, secular state of Tamil Eelam, and began clandestine support for "our boys." When the LTTE (which had changed its name from New Tamil Tigers in 1976)[2] called for a boycott of local polls in Jaffna in which the TULF participated in 1983, the turnout was only 10 percent. The TULF had been overtaken by the boys.

It is worth noting that this was not a radicalization of the marginalized or poor. Radicalization occurred, or, more accurately, militancy and separatism grew, within a minority community that was, on average, better off and better educated than the majority. That minority was being progressively dispossessed of power after being accustomed to thinking of itself as a natural ruling elite. Indian-origin Tamils and people in

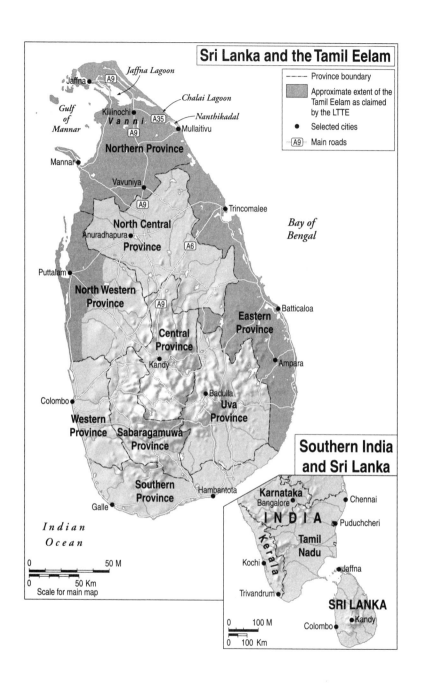

Sri Lanka and the Tamil Eelam

- - - - - Province boundary
Approximate extent of the Tamil Eelam as claimed by the LTTE
● Selected cities
A9 Main roads

Jaffna
A9
Jaffna Lagoon
Kilinochi
Vanni
A35
Chalai Lagoon
Nanthikadal
A9
Mullaitivu
Gulf of Mannar

Northern Province

Mannar
Vavuniya
A9
Trincomalee

North Central Province
Anuradhapura
A6

Bay of Bengal

Puttalam

North Western Province
A9

Eastern Province
Batticaloa

Central Province
Kandy
Ampara

Colombo
Badulla
Uva Province

Western Province
Sabaragamuwa Province

Southern Province
Hambantota
Galle

Indian Ocean

0   50 M
0   50 Km
Scale for main map

Southern India and Sri Lanka

Karnataka
Bangalore
Chennai
INDIA
Puduchcheri
Tamil Nadu
Kochi
Kerala
Jaffna
Trivandrum
SRI LANKA
Colombo
Kandy

0   100 M
0   100 Km

Tamilnadu often complained that the Jaffna Tamils had a superiority complex and looked down on them.[3] But by the 1980s a whole generation of Jaffna Tamil youth had grown up without prospects in Sri Lanka.

Opinion had also hardened on the Sinhala side. The Sinhalese saw themselves as disadvantaged by the Tamils and their English education. Ironically, both the Sri Lankan Tamils and the Sinhalese thought of themselves as threatened and behaved as threatened minorities do. In July 1983, the reaction to an LTTE ambush of an SLA checkpoint near Tirunelveli was an organized nationwide pogrom and massacre of Tamils across the country during what came to be called Black July. Anywhere between 400 and 3,000 Tamils were killed. The start of the civil war is dated to those events. Two decades of organized discrimination against the Tamils had been followed by preplanned violence. Tit-for-tat attacks on shrines, soldiers, and other groups followed with increasing frequency. Both sides thus hardened the racial and religious divide.

By the mid-1980s Velupillai Prabhakaran had made the LTTE his own. The LTTE had clearly emerged as the dominant but not yet the only Tamil separatist organization resorting to violence. Born into a middle-class family, the son of a district land officer, Prabhakaran joined student politics in school, and carried out his first political murder at the age of twenty-one in 1975. In many ways Prabhakaran's rise matches the classic theory of the rise of revolutionaries who come from marginal elements of society but are middle class themselves. He was able to mobilize lumpen elements, kill or terrify the elite, and build a revolution on expatriate and angry members of the community, putting together the money, skills, and ability to construct one of the most lethal terrorist organizations the world had seen.

By the end of the 1980s the LTTE had made itself the "sole representative" of those struggling for Tamil Eelam by the simple expedient of physically eliminating its political rivals and outdoing them in extremism. In fact, Prabhakaran first came to public attention by killing the elected and popular Tamil mayor of Jaffna, Alfred Duriappa, in 1975, setting a pattern for the future. Prabhakaran and the LTTE pioneered the use of suicide bombers on the Indian subcontinent in July 1987 when Capt. Miller of the Black Tigers drove a small truck filled with explosives into an SLA camp, killing forty soldiers. This became their trademark. They carried out more than 378 suicide attacks until 2009, including the one that killed former prime minister Rajiv Gandhi in India in May 1991.

The View from India

India had two main worries as the situation in Sri Lanka deteriorated in the mid-1980s. The first was the rise of Tamil separatism. More than 60 million Tamils live in India, and some of them had been attracted to separatist sentiment in the past, during the language riots in the 1960s in Tamilnadu against the imposition of Hindi. The fear in Delhi was that Tamil separatism would spread from Sri Lanka to Tamilnadu. As one Tamil politician told me, "Tamil Eelam does not make sense without us." The other concern was the opportunity that trouble in Sri Lanka gave outside powers to interfere in what was so far a quiet periphery, compared to the northern borders with China and Pakistan. India's external intelligence agency, the Research and Analysis Wing (RAW), was therefore tasked from the 1970s on to keep an eye on the LTTE and other groups (PLOTE, EROS, TELO, EPRLF, TELA, and so on).[4] Most accounts say that RAW also trained and supported these groups between August 1983 and May 1987. The logic was that a degree of contact and control over them would be useful to further the peaceful evolution of a solution to the Tamil problem in Sri Lanka. These hopes were dashed by the subsequent course of events. There are certainly lessons in the RAW's experience with the LTTE on the risks of using covert means and uncontrollable instruments to achieve what may appear to be laudable and moderate political ends.

Through the 1980s India tried to simultaneously mediate and use its influence with both the Tamil political groups and the Sri Lankan government to find a peaceful solution, through the devolution of powers within the Sri Lankan constitution, which would maintain Sri Lanka's unity while giving Sri Lankan Tamils a voice in their own future. Several rounds of talks brokered by India in Colombo, Delhi, and Bhutan's capital, Thimphu, failed to stop the massacres of civilians and terrorist attacks. By mid-1987 these had escalated into conventional warfare by the SLA on Sri Lankan soil. The population of Jaffna was under siege and without supplies and food. On June 5, 1987, the Indian Air Force air-dropped 25 tons of medicines and food in Jaffna, informing the Sri Lankan government only just before the action. The situation in Sri Lanka was deteriorating rapidly, and India's relations with this strategically located neighbor were at considerable risk.

The crisis clearly called for new thinking and steps by all sides.

On July 29, 1987, when Prime Minister Rajiv Gandhi visited Colombo, India and Sri Lanka came to an understanding that the Sri Lankan
government would devolve powers on the Indian model to a new merged
Northern and Eastern Province, to be called the North-East Province,
where Tamils were concentrated, and grant official status to the Tamil
language (through the 13th Amendment to the Sri Lankan Constitution). India and Sri Lanka signed an agreement that made it possible for
India to dispatch an Indian Peace Keeping Force (IPKF) to accept the sur-
render of arms by Tamil militants as part of a general cease-fire. All the
groups, including Prabhakaran personally, agreed to this. But these arrangements soon broke down.[5]

It is debatable whether the LTTE ever intended to really lay down
their arms. In any case, the Sri Lankan government had trouble in the
Sinhala south as well, where the accord provoked unrest and fueled an
insurrection by an ultra-nationalist and extreme Marxist Sinhala group,
the Janatha Vimukthi Peramuna (JVP). Before long, the IPKF was in
full-fledged combat with the LTTE in the north and east, and accusations of human rights violations were being leveled by all sides. The Indian Army has always believed that it was forced to fight in Sri Lanka
with one hand tied behind its back. Popular support for the intervention in India was not high, and the government in Colombo wavered
between those who wanted the IPKF to finish off the LTTE and those
who saw its presence as an affront to Sri Lankan sovereignty. President
Junius Richard (JR) Jayewardene, who signed the India–Sri Lanka
Agreement that brought in the IPKF, was known as the Silver Fox of
Sri Lankan politics. He used the IPKF to fight the LTTE in the north
and east, freeing up his own forces to take on the JVP insurgency[6] in
the south. His successor, President Ranasinghe Premadasa, however,
was determined to rid Sri Lanka of the foreign military presence
posed by the IPKF. He not only demanded in 1989 that the IPKF be
withdrawn but came to a secret understanding with the LTTE for a
tacit cease-fire, and even got the SLA to clandestinely give arms to the
LTTE to fight the IPKF. On March 24, 1990, the last IPKF soldier left
Sri Lanka.

It is hard to see the Indian intervention in Sri Lanka in the late 1980s
as anything but an inexorable tragedy. India had very few choices, and
no good ones, in 1987. The country was facing a deteriorating situation
in Sri Lanka, where the sharpening ethnic conflict fueled the rise of terrorism within the Tamil community, led to the flow of Tamil refugees into

India, and even saw fighting among Sri Lankan Tamil militant groups on Indian soil. At the same time, the ethnic conflict was driving the Sri Lankan government to seek weapons from, and rely on, China, Pakistan, Israel, and the United States. India was trying to improve its relations with the United States and did ultimately come to an understanding with the Reagan administration, which went along with India's intervention in Sri Lanka. But India's relations with China and Pakistan, both countries India had fought wars with, led to wariness of their influence and presence in Sri Lanka. The intervention was therefore also an attempt to preempt outside influences and not leave a vacuum for others to fill in Sri Lanka.

The bitterness left by the Indian intervention had longlasting effects. On May 21, 1991, Rajiv Gandhi was assassinated by a female LTTE suicide bomber, Thenmozhi Rajaratnam, while campaigning in Sriperumbudur, Tamilnadu. Whatever little sympathy that had remained in India for the LTTE as the underdog evaporated. Equally, there was little Indian interest in intervening militarily in Sri Lanka after the bitter IPKF experience. It could be argued that India's actions in 2009, which made Prabhakaran's end inevitable and inspired the hands-off attitude of the international community, were a direct result of that one act by Prabhakaran, whose involvement in the assassination was conclusively proved in court during the trial of the other conspirators in the Rajiv Gandhi assassination.

Massacres and Assassinations

As soon as the IPKF had left Sri Lanka, the LTTE turned on Premadasa's forces. On June 11, 1990, the LTTE massacred 600 Sri Lankan policemen, who had been disarmed after surrendering under promise of safe passage. Full-scale hostilities resumed in July, and the LTTE took over the entire north and drove out Muslims and Sinhalese from their homes in the North-East Province and the Jaffna Peninsula in October. The sight of bodies burning on the roadsides, torched by shadowy death squads formed by both Premadasa and the LTTE, became common throughout Sri Lanka. On May Day 1993, Premadasa himself was assassinated by a suicide bomber in Colombo.

The war wound on its bloody and inconclusive way in the following years. On December 5, 1995, the SLA retook Jaffna after ten years. President Chandrika Bandaranaike was elected in 1994 on the promise of a negotiated peace but ended up losing her right eye to an LTTE suicide bomber in a failed assassination attempt in December 1999. She was the one politician in Sri Lanka with a truly national vision, extending beyond her own immediate political advantage; the one politician who had the credibility with both the Sinhala and the Tamil masses needed to bring about a peaceful, negotiated settlement of the civil war and the ethnic problem at its root. But Prabhakaran was not ready to compromise. The LTTE response to peace moves in the mid to late 1990s was a series of spectacular bombings of hotels and even the Central Bank in Colombo, and the killing of remaining moderate Tamil leaders such as Neelan Thiruchelvam. By 2000 there were at least 1 million internally displaced persons in Sri Lanka. The war had torn apart the social fabric of the country, and the economy with the best World Bank human development indicators in South Asia was tottering. Chandrika Bandaranaike's solution was to tie her economy to India's through a free trade agreement, which was negotiated between 1997 and 1998, and to seek international mediation in the conflict. War fatigue was evident on both sides, and by February 2000 both the Sri Lankan government and the LTTE had asked Norway to mediate a solution.

THE WEST'S MEDIATION EFFORTS

The international community had watched the Sri Lankan conflict from the sidelines for several years. The only major power with a vital stake in the conflict was India—for domestic political reasons in Tamilnadu, and because of Sri Lanka's geopolitical location. For others, including the United States, Sri Lanka's position astride the major Indian Ocean sea-lanes was potentially significant but not an active concern so long as no other power threatened to exclusively control Sri Lanka or the sea-lanes near it. President Reagan had been content to support Rajiv Gandhi in his intervention in Sri Lanka in 1987–90.

The international environment worsened for the LTTE after the 9/11 terrorist attacks and the start of the "global war on terror." Besides, the LTTE's growing influence, which extended to taxing the expanding Sri Lankan diaspora in the West, also began to arouse concern among Western governments. According to the best estimates of the size of the Sri Lankan Tamil diaspora abroad, more than 844,000 Sri Lankan Tamils were driven out by the war, beginning with the professionals, who were soon followed by all classes of citizenry. The best estimates by recipient

Table 4-1. Estimated Sri Lankan Tamil Diaspora in the West

Canada (2007)	200,000
United Kingdom (2008)	120,000
India	100,000
France (2008)	100,000
Australia (2009)	70,000
Germany (2008)	60,000
Switzerland	50,000
The Netherlands	20,000
Norway	13,000
Denmark	9,000
Sweden	2,000

Note: Data in the table reflect internal Indian estimates around 2008–09.

country are noted in table 4-1; Canada, the United Kingdom, India, and France were the leading recipient countries.

These are sizable numbers, and fear of further radicalization of this diaspora drove Western efforts at mediation. Over time there were four mediation efforts in the Sri Lankan civil war, starting with the Indian effort in the 1980s and continuing with three efforts by Norway. All failed. Norway came closest to success in 2001, when the LTTE for the first time suggested it might be willing to settle for less than a fully independent Eelam. Cynics attribute this development to the success of the long-range reconnaissance patrols of the SLA, which took down several LTTE commanders in 2000–01. Optimists attribute it to fatigue with the war and a strong civil society peace movement. Both are right.

Six rounds of peace talks took place, in Thailand, Germany, Norway, and Japan, between September 2000 and March 2003. Both sides agreed to a federal solution and exchanged prisoners of war. On February 22, 2002, a memorandum of understanding was formalized, the Permanent Ceasefire Agreement was signed, and Norway was formally named mediator. The Sri Lanka Monitoring Mission (SLMM) was established to monitor the cease-fire.

In March 2003, however, the talks broke down, and the SLMM's function then became essentially to monitor the breakdown of the cease-fire. (Between 2003 and 2005 the SLMM recorded more than 3,000 LTTE and about 300 SLA infractions of the cease-fire. Thereafter the SLMM stopped recording infractions.) In October 2003 the LTTE issued its own proposal calling for an interim self-governing authority fully controlled by the LTTE with broad powers in the north and east. In effect, the LTTE had gone back on promises it had made to the Norwegian mediators.

There was a strong backlash in the south. A state of emergency was imposed, elections were declared, and the hard-line Mahinda Rajapaksa was elected prime minister in April 2004. In March 2004 the northern and eastern wings of the LTTE split, with a major commander from the Eastern Province, Col. Karuna, pulling about 5,000 eastern fighters out of the LTTE, with SLA support. The LTTE's internal cohesion had begun to crumble. The LTTE's response thereafter to the tsunami (when it earned international opprobrium by killing relief workers), its assassination of former foreign minister Lakshman Kadirgamar, one of the most respected Tamils in Sri Lanka and abroad, and its resumption of a suicide bombing campaign led the international community to lose hope of mainstreaming the LTTE or coming to meaningful agreements with it. By 2005, thirty-two countries had proscribed the LTTE as a terrorist organization, including the UN and the EU. The United Kingdom was among the last to do so.

Thereafter it was the military path that the LTTE had chosen that would determine the fighters' fate and lead to their destruction as an organized fighting force.

ENDGAME

The LTTE response to changed SLA tactics after 2006 was to do more of what they had done before. In December 2006 the government began an offensive in the Eastern Province, clearing and holding territory, irrespective of the cost in lives. The LTTE used 35,000 civilians as human shields to cover their steady retreat, forcing them into the jungle and finally into the LTTE's last mountain redoubt in the Eastern Province in Thoppigala, which fell in July 2007. Using their superior numbers, firepower, and air force, the SLA cleared the Eastern Province of LTTE control by July 2007, aided by the defection of the main LTTE commander in the province, Colonel Karuna,[7] who alleged that eastern fighters were not being given their due by Prabhakaran. An LTTE obdurate in defeat and a government scenting victory rebuffed Norwegian efforts to arrange safe passage or a cease-fire to spare civilians. And the international community, primarily the West and India, in the midst of the so-called global war on terror, chose not to mediate or intervene.

In September 2007 the SLA began its Northern Campaign. This steadily decimated the LTTE leadership and shrank the territory under their control. S. P. Tamilselvam, the head of the LTTE Political Wing, was killed in November 2007. A little later Col. Charles, the head of LTTE Military Intelligence, was killed in a claymore mine ambush set by a long-range reconnaissance patrol. Prabhakaran was steadily losing his most effective lieutenants and was increasingly isolated from reality.

In October 2008 the Sri Lankan government ordered international humanitarian agencies out of LTTE-controlled areas. By November 2008 more than 200,000 internally displaced persons were living in Sri Lanka as a result of the conflict, many being herded along by the LTTE. On January 2, 2009, their administrative capital, Kilinochchi, in the Northern Province, fell, and the LTTE then abandoned Jaffna to pull back into the Mullaitivu jungles. On February 5, 2009, the last Sea Tiger base at Chabi fell to the SLA. About 200,000 people were now squeezed into an area 14 kilometers square along the Vanni coast, awaiting the SLA's final assault. By late March the LTTE were confined to a few square kilometers outside the No Fire Zone, down from the 15,000 square kilometers of just three years before.

INDIA'S CHOICES IN 2009

India was naturally worried at the prospect of widespread civilian casualties when the LTTE fighters, progressively squeezed into an ever-smaller area, resorted to their standard tactic of using the civilian populace as human shields, as they had done against the Indian Peace Keeping Force in 1987–90. This tactic was hardly likely to deter a Sinhala army under Chief of Army Staff Lt.-Gen. Sarath Fonseka and President Mahinda Rajapaksa, who had victory within their grasp after a civil war lasting more than twenty-five years. For Indian policymakers, the priority was clear: to ensure that the least harm possible fell to the civilian population trapped in the midst of war, whatever their ethnicity—Tamil, Sinhala, or Muslim. This was a moral as well as a political imperative, with Indian general elections coming up in May 2009 and Tamilnadu the state that had swung the balance in the 2004 election in favor of the ruling UPA. After all, for every Tamil in Sri Lanka there were about twenty-seven Tamils in India who were emotionally affected by and invested in what happened to Tamils in Sri Lanka.

The Indian government therefore was in intense and constant touch with the Sri Lankans and President Rajapaksa, using a "troika" arrangement consisting of National Security Adviser M. K. Narayanan, Defense Secretary Vijay Singh, and myself as foreign secretary, on our side, and Defense Secretary Gothabaya Rajapaksa, Secretary to the President Lalith Weeratunga, and member of Parliament and the president's political right hand, Basil Rajapaksa, on the Sri Lankan side. (Both Basil and Gothabaya were President Mahinda Rajapaksa's brothers, which made decisionmaking easy and quick, but the decisions, once made, were also final and hard to change.) India's external affairs minister, Pranab Mukherjee, took a personal interest and was actively involved throughout, as was Prime Minister Manmohan Singh. I vividly remember the atmosphere of crisis that built up during that period, and the repeated visits to and from Colombo in the first five months of 2009. Particularly memorable were midnight visits to Colombo with Pranab Mukherjee when we flew into Colombo at 8 p.m., went straight to the Presidential Palace for a military briefing by Fonseka and a political one by President Rajapaksa, and had a long conversation exploring options until we left the palace after midnight to fly home on the Indian Air Force's Embraer jet. By mid-January 2009 the SLA and leadership were convinced that they had the measure of the LTTE as a fighting force and that victory would be theirs.

In those conversations with the Sri Lankans, we concentrated on attempting to save civilians. To prevent attacks on civilians, we asked that there be safe corridors for them to exit the fighting zone, that an amnesty policy be announced and enforced visibly, that fighter jets not be used in the conflict to strafe LTTE positions surrounded by civilians (as most of them were deliberately located by the LTTE), and so on. To their credit, while the Rajapaksas negotiated hard to avoid limitations on their ability to wage war against their mortal enemy, they did agree to allow safe passage corridors and to create safe zones for civilians in January and February. Later in March they also agreed not to use heavy-caliber weapons when the LTTE had trapped a large number of civilians with them in a tiny area along the coast in the final stages of the war. More significantly, the Rajapaksas implemented these commitments in practice.

One thing they would not agree to, however, was any understanding on keeping the LTTE leaders alive and taking them prisoner for the purpose of putting them on trial. Nor were they willing to see any form of international mediation or a cease-fire that would enable the top LTTE leadership to survive to fight another day. There were also obvious limits to what India could press for in terms of treatment of the convicted killers of Prime Minister Rajiv Gandhi, some of whom were still wanted by the law in India.

On January 21, 2009, the SLA declared a 32-square-kilometer "safe zone" between the A35 highway and the Chalai Lagoon where they said there would be no firing. However, only a trickle of civilians were able to enter the zone. The LTTE prevented them, and the no-firing commitment had been broken when the SLA suspected the LTTE of entering the zone. Instead, civilians fled and were pushed into a narrow strip between Nanthikadal and the Indian Ocean. On February 12, 2009, the SLA declared a new safe zone, 10 square kilometers, northwest of Mullaitivu, but Sri Lankan Air Force attacks in the zone continued.

At the same time, Norway and the United States were attempting to secure a cease-fire, to negotiate exile for Prabhakaran, and to explore other exit strategies that would effectively keep the LTTE alive to fight another day, politically or militarily. For politicians and leaders in India, whether in Tamilnadu or in Delhi, this was not an acceptable stance or outcome. Political leaders across the political divide in Tamilnadu knew that the only way Prabhakaran could lead Tamil Eelam would be to physically eliminate the real leaders of the Tamils who were in India, just as he had already done to other Tamil leaders in Sri Lanka. Despite differences in public posture on the issue in Tamilnadu and Delhi, there was cross-party private understanding on the basics of policy toward Sri Lanka with both the Dravida Munnetra Kazhagam (DMK) party and the All India Anna Dravida Munnetra Kazhagam (AIADMK) party, as a result of considerable hard work by Pranab Mukherjee and Narayanan, as I found when I met alone with with very senior Tamilnadu politicians in Chennai, away from the glare of publicity. Ironically, by murdering Rajiv Gandhi, the LTTE had caused a shift in broader Indian attitudes, which came to be more in line with those of the Sri Lankan government.

Limited Options

India's policy options in the situation were limited. We recognized that a victorious Rajapaksa would be less dependent on India and therefore less responsive. A consummate politician who had risen through the political ranks, pragmatic and practical to the core, Mahinda Rajapaksa by 2009 had a firm grip on all the levers of power in Sri Lanka, standing head and shoulders above his potential rivals. He also had strong military, political, and financial support for his war from China, Pakistan, and, to an extent, the United States. The United States was willing to help him in practice with intelligence and military training but was constrained to express human rights concerns, without letting them rise to the level of affecting his conduct of the war against terrorism. If India had stood aside or asked him to desist, in effect, defending the killers of an Indian prime minister, we would have effectively written ourselves out of Sri Lanka for the next decade or more, sacrificing our maritime and other interests in Sri Lanka and abdicating a geopolitically strategic neighbor to other powers. More than 90 percent of our foreign trade and most of our energy supplies came along the sea-lanes that Sri Lanka sits astride, and we could hardly abandon Sri Lanka to potentially hostile influences. In effect, Sri Lanka is an aircraft carrier parked fourteen miles off the Indian coast. This is the perpetual dilemma of India's Sri Lanka policy: we must engage in order to defend our interest in keeping Sri Lanka free of antagonistic outside influences while also trying to prevent the growth of Tamil extremism and separatism that could affect Tamilnadu. These twin objectives are not necessarily perfectly aligned. For much of the 1980s, India's humanitarian impulses and strategic interests were pulling in different directions. But by 2009 the murder of Rajiv Gandhi had made a more realistic Indian policy possible. While other states had the luxury of urging diplomacy and first principles of good conduct, in this case, India did not.

In the event, Rajapaksa, knowing that victory was around the corner, was in no mood to agree to Western cease-fire proposals or to any idea that the LTTE leadership might be evacuated to safety, even if that was the only certain way to prevent casualties among the civilians that the LTTE had driven onto the peninsula as their hostages and human shields.

Rajapaksa's obduracy was matched by Prabhakaran's. Prabhakaran was increasingly remote from reality. This was a man whose ego had grown with success, who was even worshipped in a temple on the Jaffna coast as an incarnation of the Hindu god Vishnu. By 2009 there was no one left in the LTTE leadership to tell him the truth in the last months of his life. They had either fallen by the wayside, like Anton Balasingham, the LTTE's chief negotiator and political strategist, or had been eliminated by Prabhakaran himself. And the ones who returned to him at that stage, such as Kumaran Pathmanathan,[8] were in it for what they could get out of the situation. In Kumaran Pathmanathan's case the attraction seems to have been the money that the LTTE had collected and stashed away.

THE SOCIAL COSTS OF SRI LANKA'S CIVIL WAR

The initial UN estimates were that between January and April 2009, 6,500 civilians were killed, 14,000 were injured, and more than 196,000 fled the conflict zone. On April 5 the LTTE lost several of its major military commanders in the Battle of Anandapuram. On April 19 the SLA broke through the LTTE defenses, and mayhem ensued. The LTTE drove about 30,000 civilians into the No Fire Zone and built a 3-kilometer defensive "bund," or large ditch, to confine them. The SLA began hunting for Prabhakaran, squeezed the LTTE further into 10 square kilometers, and penetrated the civilian-confining bund later that month.

On May 16 the SLA claimed victory. The next day the LTTE admitted defeat, posting on its website, "This battle has reached its bitter end. . . . We have decided to silence our guns." On May 18 the world saw pictures of Prabhakaran's corpse. A thirty-month campaign had ended a twenty-six-year civil war and wiped out one of the most lethal terrorist groups in the world.

And so Prabhakaran came to his sorry and bloody end, taking his entire family with him, including his son and wife. The pictures of him in death, taken by an SLA officer, brutal and violent as they are, were greeted with disbelief among the committed, and with relief in the rest of Sri Lanka. The video of his young son eating a biscuit and killed a few moments later caused revulsion around the world and brought home the brutality with which the Sri Lankan civil war had been conducted and ended.

When we totted up the costs of the war, they were considerable—far more than just the toll in dead, injured, and destroyed lives, which was bad enough. While estimates vary widely, initial UN estimates for those killed between 1983 and 2009 were as follow:

LTTE:	27,693
Sri Lankan Army	23,790
Indian Peace Keeping Force:	1,155
Civilians:	30,000–50,000
Total:	80,000–100,000

The final stages of the war created a little over 300,000 internally displaced persons, who were taken into camps in Vavuniya district, Northern Province. By January 2012 all the IDPs had been resettled except for 6,554 from Mullaitivu, whose land had not yet been de-mined. The war left 1.6 million land mines in the north and east. By January 2012, 1,934 square kilometers had been cleared and 127 square kilometers remained to be cleared of mines. After the war, around 5,000 Sri Lankan Tamil refugees who had fled to India since the start of the conflict in 1983 returned to Sri Lanka. About 68,152 Sri Lankan Tamil refugees still remain in India. The Sri Lankan government has also resettled or rehabilitated all the LTTE cadres in their custody except for about 400 whom they consider "hard cases."

The best estimates for the economic costs to Sri Lanka of the war are around U.S. $200 billion in direct costs (around five times Sri Lanka's GDP in 2009), not counting the opportunity costs to what was once the fastest-growing and most open economy in South Asia.

The real tragedy of the war was the destruction of Sri Lanka's composite society, something that the LTTE and Sinhala chauvinism are equally responsible for. The Sri Lanka that was left at the end of the war in May 2009 was very different from the Serendib of history that gave the world the word "serendipity." It was closer to, but worse than, the idyllic tropical isle that Bishop Reginald Heber (1783–1826) described in his poem:

What tho' the spicy breezes
Blow soft o'er Ceylon's isle;
Though every prospect pleases,
And only man is vile?

SRI LANKA'S DEMOCRACY WAS now flawed by disappearances, killings, torture, detentions, and widespread human rights abuses committed by all sides in the war. Civil-military relations were skewed, Sinhala society was militarized, and the brutalized remnants of Sri Lankan Tamil society were leaderless and without direction or hope. Nor was there any sign of an attempt to come to terms with the legacy and result of the war, to undertake real reconciliation.

In death, Prabhakaran left his Sri Lankan Tamil community gutted and brutalized by his war. The Jaffna Tamils, who had once fed, led, ruled, and thought for Ceylon, were reduced to a group of refugees in their own country and abroad, dependent on aid and the dole, their best and brightest dead or in exile. In death as in life Prabhakaran's baleful impact on his people continued to take its toll.

THE PEACE VACUUM

The first priority was rehabilitation, which had to take precedence over reconciliation. In this aspect Sri Lanka did relatively well. India helped considerably, offering to build 50,000 houses for the IDPs returning to their homes, helping with de-mining, rebuilding roads and railways in the north and east and in the south, providing immediate medical help in the camps, and helping to restart schools and other normal institutions in the north and east. Even before the fighting ended, India had set up field hospitals for the refugees and IDPs and sent relief supplies to them in early 2009. The physical scars of the war have been largely erased, and Sri Lanka can claim to have rehabilitated and restored normalcy much faster than other countries that endured shorter civil wars, such as Cambodia, Ruanda, or the United States.

But peace is more than an absence of violence and the presence of basic infrastructure. It is also in the mind. And this is where Sri Lanka has failed since the war. A victorious regime under Mahinda Rajapaksa and the Sinhala majority did not show the magnanimity in victory that true peace requires. Equally, the Tamil community does not have leaders left who can make peace. A Mandela needs a De Klerk, and vice versa. Neither is visible in Sri Lanka. In Sri Lanka, politics are stunted on both sides. Nor has either side, or the international community, managed to get past the arguments of the past. Much time has been spent on whether and how to implement the 13th Amendment to the Sri Lankan Constitution, passed after the India–Sri Lanka Agreement of 1987, which provided for the devolution of powers. How relevant those arguments of the past are today is debatable. It shows a paucity of leadership and thought that the same sterile arguments of the last thirty years on devolution and constitutional arrangements continue to dominate the political process, such as it is, between Sinhala and Tamil political parties.

On the other hand, international opinion shifted after the war to seeking a reckoning for war crimes and human rights violations. Since the LTTE had been eliminated as an organization, in practice, this meant calling the Sri Lankan government to account for its conduct of the war and its human rights violations. The United States took the lead in piloting stronger and stronger resolutions through the UN Human Rights Council (UNHRC) after the war. The March 2014 resolution, based on the findings of the UN Secretary-General's Panel of Experts, which found credible allegations of crimes by the Sri Lankan military and LTTE, asked the UNHRC to investigate the allegations.

The Sri Lankan government naturally argued that this was Sri Lanka's internal affair and that it would handle the issues itself, a position in which it received support from China, Russia, and all developing countries except India. The government set up a Lessons Learnt and Reconciliation Commission (LLRC), which reported in 2012 with a road map to address the issues—a road map that was described as insufficient by Sri Lankan Tamil parties and as too conciliatory by the Sinhala parties. It remains to be seen whether international efforts by the UNHRC and other bodies, driven partly by a radicalized Tamil diaspora in the West, will continue, now that a new government has been elected in 2015 in Colombo, replacing the Rajapaksa regime that presided over the final and most brutal phases of the war.

If reconstruction and relief were an immediate priority, the longer-term interest in preventing a resurgence of militancy and terrorism in Sri Lanka demanded reconciliation and political sagacity. Rajapaksa found this hard to do. We urged President Rajapaksa that if he truly was to be the leader of all Sri Lankans, he should reach out through devolution of political power and democratic means, restoring human rights and a sense of dignity to victor and vanquished alike in his country. While he facilitated India's reconstruction and relief work, Rajapaksa could not bring himself to be politically magnanimous in victory. To some extent he was correct in telling us that there was no one he could work with on the Tamil side. Such Tamil politicians as had survived the war in the Tamil National Alliance were either complicit with or indebted to the LTTE and the most radical elements in the diaspora. But Rajapaksa did not use his effective and overwhelming power to promote a moderate Tamil leadership. Instead he relied on turncoat Tamil militants like Douglas Devananda and his EPDP (Eelam People's Democratic Party) muscle power, and deployed fourteen of his twenty-one SLA divisions in the north, in large military zones expropriated from Tamils, thus appearing as an occupying power rather than as the legitimate government of the people.

The other postwar issue that worried India was the civil-military balance after twenty-six years of civil war in Sri Lanka. This was solved expeditiously if unconventionally by sacking and imprisoning army chief Sarath Fonseka. Fonseka's political ambitions were the real motive behind Rajapaksa's action, but the effect of removing him was to take out of politics the victorious and domineering army, which had got used to playing a role in national politics. Rajapaksa gave effective command of the army to his brother Gothabaya, a former military officer who was the defense secretary. Gothabaya was already determining all significant postings and military decisions during the last few years of the war and is not shy of claiming credit for victory, as the book *Gota's War* makes clear.[9]

I found that as defense secretary, Gothabaya had a clear view of Sri Lanka's interests, one that was compatible with ours. Immediately after the war, he reassured the Indian troika about the nature of Sri Lanka's defense relationship with China, and helped Indian companies reenter the reconstruction of Colombo. Security was Gothabaya's sole preoccupation, which made him sensitive to India's concerns, while his brother Mahinda was much more compliant with Chinese demands, having built a political machine on Chinese money. The basic assurances that Gothabaya and, more reluctantly, Mahinda Rajapaksa gave us were that India's security interests would be respected and that there would be no surprises in Sri Lanka's relations with China. In detailed conversations I was assured that there would be no permanent Chinese military presence in Sri Lanka, and that Sri Lanka would look to India for most of its military training and intelligence needs. These assurances were respected in practice by the Sri Lankans until May 2014. At no stage was exclusivity sought or promised. And realistically speaking, it would be unreasonable to expect exclusivity. For Sri Lanka, as for India's other smaller neighbors, using China to get India to pay attention and invest in the relationship and using India to get Chinese investment and support is a productive strategy, empirically proven in the past. For India not to recognize and deal with this fact of international life would be foolish.

THE SRI LANKAN CIVIL war is one of the few instances I can think of where terrorism (but not separatism) was successfully eradicated by purely military means. It is arguable that some brutality was inevitable in a war of this kind, against a violent terrorist group that had shown no qualms about terrorizing its own people and physically eliminating all its potential adversaries, Tamil or Sinhala. Indeed, one must logically ask the question, would an earlier adoption of the more brutal methods of the last thirty months of the war have brought it to an earlier end and actually have saved lives and minimized the war's deleterious effects? (This is a recurring problem in statecraft. It is also the strongest justification for the use of atomic weapons to end World War II.) The strategist Edward Luttwak argues that there are situations in which one should "give war a chance."[10] Was Sri Lanka one of them, where peacebuilding efforts and international mediation only prolonged and worsened the agony? These are difficult counterfactuals that go against the grain of liberal thinking, but they do seem appropriate to the Sri Lankan case.

To my mind it was a conjunction of factors, not just the conduct of the war and the use of force, that brought about the defeat of the LTTE. The international community's disenchantment with the LTTE after 2005, and India's responses after the LTTE assassinated former prime minister Rajiv Gandhi, held the ring enabling the political, military, and social isolation of the LTTE and Prabhakaran. Finally, Prabhakaran and the LTTE's inability to innovate or change in response to the new SLA tactics and the shifting environment after 2005 brought about their end in Sri Lanka.

For us in India, looking back, was there any way in which the brutality of the war's end could have been avoided or minimized further? In retrospect it is hard to see how the war could have ended in victory with less bloodshed. Nor has anyone suggested other steps that the government of India could have realistically taken. An LTTE victory would have resulted in a much greater bloodbath. A stalemate would only have prolonged the bloodletting. As it was, our concerted efforts, with some help from the international community, had ensured that the war ended quickly and with no more brutality than other civil wars that had reached the point of a military decision. The immediate reaction in Tamilnadu, which was voting in the Indian general election at the same time in April–May 2009, seemed to bear this assessment out. The war in Sri Lanka and the government of India's response did not prevent the DMK from taking an overwhelming majority of Lok Sabha seats in Tamilnadu, despite the disadvantages of incumbency and its membership of the ruling coalition in Delhi. Those of us who were involved in policy on the Indian side will feel that we did what we could. Whether it was enough must remain a matter of opinion.

This was also one of the longest civil wars in history, which only heightened its impact—political, psychological and in other ways. While rehabilitation was possible and fast, reconciliation has been virtually impossible. And as time passes it seems less likely that there will be a reckoning that satisfies all concerned. The world is ready to move on, as are the victors, the Sinhala. But the Tamil sense of grievances unaddressed makes the return of separatism and radicalism in another form a matter of time, in my view. Much will depend on how politics and society develop in Tamilnadu, the true land of the Tamils, in the years ahead. For the present there is declared sympathy but little real support in Tamilnadu for the causes or the methods that the LTTE adopted.

THE DILEMMAS OF STATECRAFT

If this rather long and detailed account of a protracted civil war the world ignored has given some idea of the complexity of foreign policy decision-making, it will have served a purpose. For the Sri Lankan civil war is an example of several dilemmas of statecraft. In Sri Lanka in 2009 the Indian government and the world were faced with an impossible choice between reasons of state and humanitarian instincts, between idealism and self-interest, between intervention and allowing a war to run its course. As a democracy, India chose to try to find a middle way between them, to try to satisfy both, in the event not fully satisfying either. Finding an outcome that was both morally and strategically satisfying in all respects was not possible. Governments are usually forced to make minimax foreign policy decisions—decisions aimed at minimizing the harm to one's own interests while maximizing the gain. Whether you succeed or not is never apparent at the moment, nor is it necessarily clear subsequently. Politics is a process, without clear mathematical solutions or distinctions between right and wrong, true and false, black and white. That is one reason for the growing industry of memoirs and history writing. Using Reinhold Niebuhr's definition, politics is inevitably tragic, that things do not get into politics unless they are otherwise irreconcilable, that there are no "solutions" that meet everyone's demands or interests.[11]

At the same time, it is worth remembering what Hannah Arendt said, which makes it clear that the primary responsibility lies in the internal politics of Sri Lanka rather than with international relations or the foreign policy choices of major powers. She observed that the idea of human rights, such as the right to democratic standing and political change, is a chimera and a cruel taunt without a political community that can make it good through robust institutions and practices.[12] The state of Sri Lanka in 2009 showed that the world is far from being such a polity, or a federation of such polities, and also showed just how much is at stake in their absence. But no matter what one might think of its internal politics, Sri Lanka today is a better place without the LTTE and the civil war. And India contributed to making that outcome possible.

CHAPTER FIVE

Why India Pledges No First Use of Nuclear Weapons

One sword keeps another in the sheath.
— GEORGE HERBERT, *Outlandish Proverbs,* 1640

A road is made by walking.
—Indian proverb

I AM OFTEN ASKED why India committed itself to not using its nuclear weapons first. The center-right National Democratic Alliance (NDA) government adopted the no-first-use doctrine when India first publicly tested nuclear weapons at Pokhran in 1998, and all subsequent governments of India have reiterated this pledge.[1] The doctrine states that:

> The fundamental purpose of Indian nuclear weapons is to deter the use and threat of use of nuclear weapons by any State or entity against India and its forces. India will not be the first to initiate a nuclear strike, but will respond with punitive retaliation should deterrence fail.

> India will not resort to the use or threat of use of nuclear weapons against States which do not possess nuclear weapons, or are not aligned with nuclear weapon powers.

There is still some residual anxiety in India about the wisdom of this commitment, particularly in military minds. Why have a weapon and forswear its use? India could have followed the United States and Pakistan in retaining the option of using its most powerful weapon first should the nation's defense require it.

The answer to that question lies in India's nuclear doctrine, which is itself a product of the unique circumstances in which India finds itself. Those circumstances also explain why India chose to test nuclear weapons and become a declared nuclear weapon state (NWS) in 1998.

By the late 1990s, India was in a situation where two of its neighbors with whom India had fought wars after independence, Pakistan and China, were already armed with nuclear weapons and were working together to build their capabilities and proliferate them in Asia. The international nonproliferation regime was not in any position to address this problem. India therefore chose to become a declared NWS in 1998. The Indian government made that decision in the face of opposition by all the major powers, despite misgivings within Indian society, and after twenty-four years of international nuclear sanctions resulting from India's first nuclear test, Pokhran-I, in 1974. (India described the 1974 test as a "peaceful nuclear explosion," adopting a term from the Nuclear Non-Proliferation Treaty, whereas the 1988 test was described by the government of India as a nuclear weapon test.) Those sanctions had been designed to "cap, cease and roll back" India's civil nuclear program and potential to make atomic weapons. They had failed to do so. Since 1974, India had also been threatened with nuclear weapons at least three times: twice by Pakistan and once, implicitly, by the entry of the nuclear-armed U.S. aircraft carrier USS *Enterprise* into the Bay of Bengal during the 1971 war with Pakistan. (The *Enterprise* had also entered the Indian Ocean in 1962 when India and China fought their brief border war, but that move was intended to support, not threaten, India.)

When India decided to test nuclear weapons publicly, in 1998, it was evident that nuclear weapons, because of the scale and duration of the destruction they cause, are primarily political weapons, the currency of power in the nuclear age, rather than effective warfighting weapons. The government of India therefore declared after the 1998 tests that these weapons were to prevent nuclear threat and blackmail, and that India would not be the first to use nuclear weapons against other states. If, however, anyone dared use nuclear weapons against us, we would assuredly retaliate and inflict unacceptable damage on the adversary. This is India's doctrine of credible minimum deterrence. Assured retaliation combined with a no-first-use policy also means that it is not the number of nuclear weapons that India or its adversaries possess that matters. What matters is India's ability to inflict unacceptable damage in a retaliatory strike or strikes. That is what determines India's nuclear weapons posture.

In other words, India has nuclear weapons for the contribution they make to its national security in an uncertain and anarchic world by preventing others from attempting nuclear blackmail and coercion against India. Unlike in certain other NWS, India's nuclear weapons are not meant to redress a military balance, or to compensate for some perceived inferiority in conventional military terms, or to serve some tactical or operational military need on the battlefield.

These weapons have served their expected purpose. The occasions before 1998 when other powers used the explicit or implicit threat of nuclear weapons to try to change India's behavior have not been repeated since. That they did not succeed before 1998 was because of the hard-headed leadership India was fortunate to have. Since India became a declared NWS in 1998 it has not faced credible threats of that kind. So the possession of nuclear weapons has, empirically speaking, deterred others from attempting nuclear coercion or blackmail against India.

When India carried out nuclear weapons tests in May 1998, twenty-four years after first displaying the capability to do so, in May 1974, it also became the first NWS to publicly announce and debate a nuclear doctrine rapidly thereafter. That it was able to do so owed much to the preparatory thinking and work of a remarkable handful of people such as Krishnaswamy Subrahmanyam and Brajesh Chandra Mishra, most of them self-taught innovators who thought through nuclear security issues in the Indian context while in government.

A no-first-use policy was not always the natural or easy choice. I remember then Atomic Energy Commission chairman Raja Ramanna and Chief of Army Staff Krishnaswami Sundarji often talking over a drink in the mid-1980s about a future India with nuclear weapons. For Sundarji, the attraction of an Indian atom bomb was its possible military use to neutralize Chinese conventional superiority. As a physicist, Ramana was keenly aware of the limitations on use and of the practical effects of the bomb. He therefore saw it as an enabler and equalizer, not necessarily as a military weapon to be used but as a weapon the threat of whose use would enable the achievement of political and military goals. Over time, as India's conventional military position improved, Sundarji's considerations became less compelling. By the late 1990s, it was the advocates of no first use, including defense analyst K. Subrahmanyam, who prevailed and whose views were found politically most acceptable by the political leadership, particularly Prime Minister Atal Bihari Vajpayee, a longtime advocate of nuclear weapons for India with a larger vision of peace on the Indian subcontinent and in the extended neighborhood.

The no-first-use policy and assured retaliation concept naturally had several direct implications for India's nuclear strategy and posture:

- For one, it became essential that India develop a genuine delivery triad on land, sea, and air as soon as possible, to ensure survivability of its second-strike capability and to assure retaliation.

- Matching the number of warheads and missiles that India's adversaries possessed became less important than the reliability and survivability of India's own weapons. (This is relevant today when, by all accounts, Pakistan is building new plutonium-producing reactors and a large reprocessing plant and is rapidly increasing the rate of manufacture of nuclear warheads.) While first strike equals aggression, no first use equals deterrence. And deterrence requires the minimum number of weapons to make the threat of retaliation credible—in other words, credible minimum deterrence. India can thus escape an expensive arms race in nuclear weapons while safeguarding its own security.

- As these were weapons of deterrence rather than warfighting weapons, it became crucial that India's adversaries believed they would be used if certain thresholds were crossed.

- For the same reason, calibrated or proportional responses and deterrence were not the preferred posture in the initial stages of the weapons program, for it might tempt adversaries to test the space available below the threshold for full nuclear retaliation, as indeed occurred in the Kargil conflict in 1999. Instead, the logical posture at first was counter-value targeting, or targeting the opponent's assets, rather than counter-force targeting, which concentrates on the enemy's military and command structures. Nuclear-armed Prithvi missiles with their limited range of 350 kilometers were effective deterrents in our situation, since the only real targets for them are the cities of the Pakistani Punjab.

- If you rule out first use of nuclear weapons, you need to possess other means to deal with non-nuclear threats and challenges.

Interestingly, as expressed, India's doctrine is closest to the declared Chinese doctrine. Like India, China had declared a (somewhat more hedged) no-first-use policy after testing an atom bomb in 1964. After toying in the late 1980s with a shift to tactical nuclear weapons, China reversed that decision in the mid-1990s. Since 1964 China has accepted a huge asymmetry in the numbers of its nuclear weapons compared to those of its main potential adversaries, the United States and the Soviet Union/Russia. China has concentrated instead on the survivability of its arsenal to assure retaliation. Even today, China accepts that asymmetry in numbers while working on the quality, reach, and certainty of its nuclear deterrent force. In recent years China has concentrated on making technical improvements to its nuclear arsenal, such as by putting multiple independently targetable warheads on one missile or making them maneuverable during reentry. China also produces nuclear-class missiles in vast numbers, equipping them with precision guided munitions as well, to confuse the adversary and maximize strategic deception. China has so far not made a direct nuclear threat against India, as one would expect from a country that does not regard its nuclear arsenal as a warfighting weapon and enjoys superiority in conventional military terms.

There is, however, a clear difference between India's nuclear doctrine and Pakistan's. In the red lines that Lt. Gen. Khalid Kidwai, the head of the Pakistan Army's Strategic Plans Division, made known, for instance,[2] Pakistan clearly wants India to believe that it will use its nuclear weapons for tactical military uses if certain thresholds are crossed, and tries to convince India that the threshold is so low as to deter meaningful conventional operations against Pakistan by the Indian Army. During the annual Azm-e-Nau exercises in recent years Pakistan has signaled to India that it is prepared to use nuclear weapons against Indian forces if they are on Pakistani territory (as a counter to India's alleged "Cold Start" strategy).

THE PURPOSE OF A NO-FIRST-USE NUCLEAR WEAPONS POLICY

There has been debate in India over whether the country's no-first-use commitment adds to or detracts from deterrence. Successive Indian governments that have reviewed the question repeatedly since 1998 have been of the view that a no-first-use policy enhances India's deterrence efforts.

India's situation and approach are very different from those of the United States. The United States saw its problem as not just deterring the Soviet Union but figuring out how to deter conventional and nuclear aggression against exposed allies confronting local conventional inferiority. In other words, the United States was to provide extended deterrence to its allies. The United States therefore distinguishes between first strike and first use of nuclear weapons and argues for preemption in self-defense. Most U.S. scholars would argue that a no-first-use or a first-use policy is neither inherently destabilizing nor stabilizing, and that the effect of either would depend on the country's capabilities and adversaries. For India, on the other hand, the country's geographic and strategic situation meant that nuclear weapons were not seen as the answer to problems of conventional defense. India's problem has been how to deter Pakistan's or others' first use of nuclear weapons against India and further attempts at nuclear blackmail to change India's policies.

What are the alternatives to no first use? Announcing that India would strike first if it considered it necessary, as Pakistan and the United States do? Some say that our declaration is already meaningless as it is only a pious hope and does not cover other NWS. If it is meaningless, why the fuss? But that aside, a first-strike doctrine is surely destabilizing, and does not further the primary purpose of our weapons of deterring blackmail, threat, or use of nuclear weapons by an adversary against India. It is hard to see how it would. As for other contingencies, there are ways for India to handle them other than by using nuclear weapons. India's nuclear weapons are to deter other countries' use of nuclear weapons; hence the no-first-use commitment is to nuclear weapon states (NWS). There is a potential gray area as to when India would use nuclear weapons first against another NWS. Circumstances are conceivable in which India might find it useful to strike first, for instance, against an NWS that had declared it would certainly use its weapons, and if India were certain that adversary's launch was imminent. But India's present public nuclear doctrine is silent on this scenario.

Another idea that is often mentioned as an alternative to no first use is proportionate responses to a nuclear attack. There is nothing in the present doctrine that prevents India from responding proportionately to a nuclear attack, from choosing a mix of military and civilian targets for its nuclear weapons. The doctrine speaks of punitive retaliation. The scope and scale of retaliation are in the hands of the Indian leadership. Besides, what is a proportionate response to weapons of mass destruction except other weapons of mass destruction? So it is not clear what the advocates of proportionate response are really asking for. These are weapons of mass destruction whether one chooses to call them tactical or strategic, and with its no-first-use doctrine, India has reserved the right to choose how much, where, and when to retaliate. This is an awesome responsibility for any political leader, but it is the price of leadership and cannot be abdicated to a mechanical or mathematical formula or a set of strategic precepts.

No first use is a useful commitment to make if we are to avoid wasting time and effort on a nuclear arms race, such as that between the United States and Soviet Union, which produced thousands of nuclear weapons and missiles and economically contributed to the collapse of the Soviet Union. In our geography, the use of nuclear weapons as weapons of war is hardly useful militarily. For nine months of the year prevailing winds on the India-Pakistan border are westerly, and population densities on both sides of the border guarantee that there is little distinction in effect and practice between the use of tactical or strategic nuclear weapons in the India-Pakistan context. I recall that the Pakistan Army started talking of developing and using tactical nuclear weapons in response to India's alleged Cold Start doctrine for conventional forces only when there was a real risk of the Pakistan Army losing its internal and external relevance and when Gen. Musharraf seemed close to settling the Kashmir situation and taking some steps against jihadi terrorists. If there was a real fear of a Cold Start strategy among Pakistan Army strategists, it is hard to understand the steady move of Pakistani forces away from the Indian border and toward performing internal security and other functions in western Pakistan since 2004. As Pakistan's is the only nuclear weapons program in the world controlled exclusively by the military, it is also likely that sheer institutional momentum and interests led to decisions by Pakistan to increase the number of its warheads and to develop and deploy "tactical" nuclear weapons, despite the problems of command and control of these weapons, which must be devolved down the military chain of command, and the limited military utility of nuclear weapons against India in the specific India-Pakistan context. Other recent Pakistani decisions, such as setting up separate strategic forces commands for the country's air force and navy,[3] also seem to be similarly driven by service and institutional interests rather than by rational calculations of national interest.

Since India's doctrine is based on no first use, our posture and nuclear arsenal have to survive a first strike by any enemy or potential combination of adversaries. Hence India's decision to go in for a triad of delivery systems, by land, sea, and air. Once the SSBN Arihant, the nuclear-powered ballistic missile submarine, is fully commissioned, the triad will be in place. Today, India has effective deterrence against both China and Pakistan. This has been a huge and largely secret effort, and has been achieved by India faster than by any other NWS. We are sometimes accused of excessive secrecy in relation to our own people and scholars. That is because the purpose of the nuclear weapons program is to deter our adversaries, not our own people or scholars. And our adversaries will in any case believe what they think they have discovered and ferreted out, not what we say in public. Of course, we will be most convincing if what we say matches what they find out for themselves.

Reducing Vulnerability to Nuclear Threats in the Neighborhood

At the broadest level, the decision to go overtly nuclear in 1998 has been vindicated by our experience since then. These weapons were meant to prevent nuclear coercion and blackmail. They have actually done so. Not having been deterred by nuclear threats in 1971, 1987, or 1990 from following its course when it was in a much weaker position, India's overt nuclear weapons status makes the nation less vulnerable to such threats today. But how does that work itself out in practice?

INDIA-CHINA DETERRENCE

India-China nuclear deterrence is stable and will likely remain so despite shifts leading to equilibrium at higher technological levels as both programs develop increasing sophistication. So far India and China have not bilaterally discussed their nuclear weapons and their effect on the bilateral relationship or on each other's security. This is understandable as it is only recently that India has begun to acquire the means to establish nuclear deterrence vis-à-vis China. Nor have nuclear weapons figured in their bilateral exchanges even in moments of considerable tension, whether during the 1967 border clashes in Sikkim, when China was a declared NWS; in 1986 during the Sumdorong Chu crisis, when India was believed to be in a "recessed deterrent" posture and assumed to have some nuclear weapons; or thereafter as the bilateral relationship has eased. There is, however, third-party interest (in Pakistan and the United States) in getting discussions going on strategic stability between and among India, China, and Pakistan, including discussions about their nuclear weapons. Both China and India have so far resisted entering into such discussions, though China's opposition will weaken as that nation increasingly seeks to lead or make a new security order in Asia to fit its needs. India has so far not seen such discussions as contributing to its security, or even to certainty about the actions of either Pakistan or China, thus building confidence.

Besides, the very idea of strategic stability as a goal among these three countries, or in the Asia-Pacific region in general, makes little sense when the balance of power is changing so rapidly and several powers—China, India, Vietnam, South Korea, Indonesia—are rising and rapidly accumulating power. In a region where the institutions of consultation and negotiation on security issues are underdeveloped, strategic stability sounds to emerging powers like an attempt to continue an untenable status quo by those who designed and manage the present security order in Asia. Instead, only an approach and an order that recognize that present realities are changing and will keep changing for some time to come have any chance of success. Hence it is processes and institutions to manage changing security dynamics that will have the most chance of success, in my opinion.

As for the specifics of India's situation vis-à-vis China, these will continue to change as both countries' programs evolve. Even though the primary drivers of China's nuclear weapons program may be the U.S. posture and extended deterrence in Asia, Chinese developments have direct implications for Indian security and affect India's nuclear posture.

An example is China's decision to move rapidly ahead to add MIRV (multiple independently targeted reentry vehicle) systems to its missiles. This technological tweaking affects strategic stability and deterrence in Asia and the world, as does China's decision to test anti-satellite weapons. Should all the affected powers react individually, taking measures to counter or mitigate the threat, the result will be increased systemic instability and increased insecurity all around. If they act together, or seem to, it will feed China's fear of encirclement and justify an accelerated Chinese anti-satellite program, bringing about precisely the outcome that other powers wish to prevent. What is happening today is the former, and this only increases uncertainty.

The other factor guiding the Indian calculus of deterrence is the assistance that China has consistently given Pakistan's missile and nuclear programs, both civilian and for weapons, since 1976. This is the only known instance of an NWS creating and sustaining another one in its neighborhood. It is difficult to see how this adds to China's security except as an outside check on India in a long-term game of wei chi—"encirclement chess"—better known by its Japanese name, Go. The Chinese assumed after the first Indian nuclear tests of 1974 that India had followed their example in deciding to build nuclear weapons but had chosen to do so clandestinely. Deng Xiaoping and the Chinese People's Liberation Army (PLA) newspaper *Liberation Army Daily* referred to six NWS states in the late 1980s, mentioning India as one of them. Chinese assistance to Pakistan's nuclear weapons program began in June 1976, communicated by Mao Zedong to Zulfikar Ali Bhutto, and was not disowned or stopped as a leftist aberration, as it could have been if China had wished, after Mao's death and the fall of his chosen successors, the Gang of Four and Hua Guofeng. The longevity of the intimate relationship between the two nuclear weapons programs over forty years, outlasting changes in regime and political orientation in both China and Pakistan, is truly remarkable.

Since the 1970s, Pakistani engineers like A. Q. Khan, founder of Pakistan's uranium enrichment program, have provided China with access to Western nuclear and military technology when it was unavailable to China. China in turn has shared with Pakistan its experience of testing and manufacturing nuclear weapons and has given Pakistan the technological means to deliver them. There has never been a clear stop to this collaboration, which now extends to Pakistan's quest to acquire SSBNs (an initialism for "ship submersible ballistic nuclear," or ballistic missile–equipped submarines with nuclear warheads), to develop and deploy tactical nuclear weapons, and to place nuclear warheads on its cruise and other missiles.

From the Indian point of view the Chinese and Pakistani nuclear weapons programs are so closely linked and have been so for so long that they may effectively be treated as one. This is why Prime Minister Vajpayee's letter to U.S. President Bill Clinton about the May 1998 tests mentioned explicitly that China had "materially helped another neighbour of ours to become a covert nuclear weapons state." The United States promptly leaked the text of the letter, and the loss of face occasioned by this public calling out may have contributed to the venomous

Chinese reaction to the Indian tests, as the United States probably intended. It remains the case that China's nuclear weapons are a major strategic concern for India, the Pakistani program remains a daily source of tactical worry, and their connection magnifies both manyfold.

INDIA-PAKISTAN DETERRENCE

There are several issues about India-Pakistan deterrence post-1998, particularly after the 2001–03 buildup and confrontation. Pakistan has consistently sought to use nuclear deterrence to permit that country to undertake actions against India, in Jammu and Kashmir state and elsewhere.

As the Kargil War showed, Pakistan miscalculated when it thought in 1999, one year after the tests, that its nuclear weapons would deter India from responding with conventional military force to Pakistan's intrusion across the Line of Control[4] and would bring India and the world to the negotiating table. Neither expectation was fulfilled. India retaliated militarily using its conventional superiority to clear the heights that Pakistani troops had occupied. And Pakistan's allies, China and the United States, intervened diplomatically, pressuring Pakistan to respect the Line of Control and withdraw its forces, even though they were disguised as mujahideen.

However, it is only slowly being generally recognized in Pakistan and is certainly not acknowledged by the Pakistan Army that the Kargil War ended in military and diplomatic failure for Pakistan. Indeed, the Pakistan Army seems to have drawn the conclusion that India's decision to respect the Line of Control (born out of a desire to legitimize the Line of Control) was a result of Pakistan's nuclear deterrence working to prevent an Indian riposte elsewhere or an escalation to full-scale conventional hostilities, thus limiting the conflict to Pakistan's advantage.

If the lessons learned by the Pakistan Army from Kargil were wrong, the army's practice suggests it may have drawn a more dangerous conclusion still. The Pakistan Army seems to believe that Pakistan's nuclear shield permits Pakistan to undertake terrorist attacks on India without fear of retaliation. This may well have figured in the Pakistan Army's calculations behind the Mumbai attack of November 26, 2008. The Pakistan Army could believe that its nuclear threats in 1987 during the Brasstacks exercises and during the 1990 Kashmir crisis worked and prevented Indian military retaliation. Again after the 2008 terrorist attack on Mumbai, which had clearly been mounted from Pakistan with ISI support, the lack of an overt Indian military response may have confirmed the Pakistan Army in this belief.

Since the Mumbai attacks, the Pakistan Army has extended its proactive nuclear doctrine in practice to building what it calls tactical nuclear weapons and their delivery systems, such as the short 60-kilometer-range Nasr missile. As the former head of the Pakistan Army Strategic Plans Division (that is, their strategic forces command) has explained, Pakistan is creating "full spectrum deterrence" against India, plugging the tactical level gap that allows shallow Indian penetrations into Pakistan territory with tactical nuclear weapons.[5] What this means is that Pakistan will build many more nuclear warheads and that use of these so-called tactical weapons will be devolved to several lower-ranking officers at the battlefield level. Once that happens, command and control of these lethal weapons will be much looser. The decision to use these weapons will be in the hands of many more young officers in an army that is increasingly religiously motivated and less and less professional, and that has consistently produced rogue officers and staged coups against its own leaders, starting with the Rawalpindi Conspiracy of 1950, which sought to depose the first prime minister of Pakistan.[6] Pakistan claims to seek to integrate its conventional and nuclear warfighting plans and capabilities even more closely, thinking that this will increase its immunity from Indian retaliation. But the actual consequences are to diminish deterrence stability between India and Pakistan, to bring the likelihood of nuclear war closer, and ultimately to destabilize the Pakistan Army itself.

What is the answer to this Pakistani belief in Pakistan's immunity from retaliation against terrorism and other asymmetric attacks against India, thanks to its having a nuclear deterrent? One response would be to revise India's nuclear doctrine and strategy to a warfighting one, developing tactical nuclear weapons and threatening to use them. But this shift would be reactive and would not increase the effectiveness of deterrence. Instead it would add one more level of complexity and bring nuclear war closer. Nor would such a shift be credible. An army that so misread the lessons of Kargil is hardly likely to draw the right conclusions from a change in India's statements. It could regard the shift as a verbal change until India actually carried out a nuclear first strike or a demonstration strike on Pakistan. The democratic leadership of a country like India is unlikely to use nuclear weapons against another country except in extremis. To threaten that a terrorist attack from Pakistan on India would be answered by the use of nuclear weapons would be like threatening to kill a mosquito with a shotgun and would be unlikely to be understood by India's own people, let alone the international community. What would be credible would be the message India conveyed by how it configures its forces.

If Pakistan were to use tactical nuclear weapons against India, even against Indian forces in Pakistan, it would effectively be opening the door to a massive Indian first strike, having crossed India's declared red lines. There would be little incentive, once Pakistan had taken hostilities to the nuclear level, for India to limit its response, since that would only invite further escalation by Pakistan. India would hardly risk giving Pakistan the chance to carry out a massive nuclear strike after the Indian response to Pakistan using tactical nuclear weapons. In other words, Pakistani tactical nuclear weapon use would effectively free India to undertake a comprehensive first strike against Pakistan.

In addition, the answer to non-nuclear asymmetric threats must lie in a strategy of multiple flexible responses outside the nuclear end of the spectrum of conflict. In Pakistan's particular case, this would require a deliberate strategy of containment, which raises the costs of terrorism as a state policy to Pakistan, the Pakistan Army, and the jihadi tanzeems (groups) on a long-term basis. There are several responses short of war available to a state like India.

It seems to me that rather than seeking answers in our nuclear weapons to all the threats that India does or may face, it is important that we maintain the fundamentals of our doctrine, treating our nuclear weapons as political instruments that deter nuclear attack and attempts at coercion. The clearer and simpler the task of our nuclear weapons, the more credible they are. And the more credible they are, the stronger will be their deterrent effect.

As for non-nuclear threats, there are other ways of dealing with them that are not beyond Indian ingenuity and capability to discover. Each portion of the spectrum must be dominated and shaped by India independently, if we are to deter attacks and, should deterrence fail, control the escalation of the conflict thereafter. Those are the capabilities that we build and work on.

There are, of course, several other issues related to India's nuclear strategy. They include the effects on deterrence of the ballistic missile defenses that both Pakistan and China are trying to build; the risks of unauthorized use of nuclear weapons or of them falling into terrorist hands as the Pakistani state weakens, leaving a stronger army to dominate society; command, control, and custody issues when nuclear weapons are treated as warfighting weapons, as Pakistan so treats them; and potential nuclear and missile proliferation in India's extended neighborhood. Each of these affects India's security directly and will require analysis and responses in our nuclear strategy. If we can do what we have done so far, which is to think for ourselves and devise our own doctrines and solutions to problems, developing a nuclear strategy that is uniquely Indian, I am sure we will be successful in dealing with these questions as well.

DETERRENCE IN THE INDIAN OCEAN

Another dimension of India's nuclear posture that will gain increasing importance in the future is the maritime dimension, primarily in the Indian Ocean. As a result of the no-first-use commitment, it is critical for the credibility of India's deterrence that India's nuclear weapons survive any conceivable first strike by an adversary. And the best way known today of ensuring survivability is to locate these weapons at sea, on submarines. In July 2009 India launched the INS Arihant, a nuclear-propelled submarine with the capability of firing missiles with nuclear warheads, or submarine-launched ballistic missiles (SLBMs).

The Indian Ocean has been nuclearized since the late Cold War years, when the United States used the vastness of this ocean and the difficulty of tracking submarines in its open geography to locate some of its submarines targeting Russia with nuclear weapons. (In this respect the Indian Ocean is very different from the seas near China and Russia, all of which have only a few egress points through narrow straits, which can be monitored for sound to reveal the passage of submarines even if they are submerged. It has thus been theoretically possible for the United States to track Chinese and Russian SSBNs for several decades, thus reducing their efficacy as deterrent weapons and leading them to seek other solutions.) For us, the open geography of the Indian Ocean means that if we were to track Chinese nuclear submarines, we would need to do so from their points of egress from the South China Sea or East China Sea through the first island chain, not just at the Malacca Straits but at Lombok, Sunda, and other entrances to the Indian Ocean. With Pakistan, India would attempt to know when Pakistan's SSBNs left their home ports of Karachi or Gwadar and to track them continuously thereafter. The same would be true of other possible entrants into this group, such as Iran.

These are no longer theoretical considerations for India. Since 2013, the PLA navy deployments to the Indian Ocean Region have become normal, as they have been in the Western Pacific beyond the first island chain since 2010. The PLA has been engaged in counterpiracy in the Gulf of Aden since 2008. And in 2014 a Chinese SSBN entered the Indian Ocean for the first time, followed by two more visits the same year. Technology and evolving Chinese military strategy are tending toward the offensive, toward forward deployments and toward preemption.

Pakistan announced in 2012 that it was raising a naval strategic forces headquarters and declared its intent to develop a sea-based deterrent. The Pakistani strategy appears to be to disperse a variety of low-yield nuclear weapons across naval platforms. Pakistan says that it seeks escalation dominance, strategic depth, and deterrence against a preemptive first strike. To do so it opts for dual-use platforms and strategic ambiguity.

All in all, no other NWS faces as complex a combination of factors in its deterrence calculus as India. And it is the uniqueness of India's situation that explains the uniqueness of India's nuclear doctrines and postures.

India's Advocacy of a Nuclear Weapon–Free World

There is one other aspect as well in which India's situation is unique. India is the only NWS that is a full-throated advocate of nuclear disarmament. It is also the only NWS to have waited twenty-four years after demonstrating the ability to make and explode nuclear weapons before declaring itself an NWS.

The apparent paradox of India as an NWS advocating a nuclear weapon free–world is simply explained. We do think that we would be more secure in a world that is truly free of nuclear weapons. But until we arrive at that happy state, we have no choice, and a responsibility toward our own people, to have nuclear weapons to protect them from nuclear threats.

The question is how India's disarmament and nonproliferation positions should change now that India is a declared NWS, recognized as such in practice by most of the international community. There are two issues here. One is the presentational one, whereby India is accused of freeloading on existing regimes without joining them. That has largely been put behind us by adherence to international control regimes, such as the Nuclear Suppliers Group requirements, the Missile Technology

Control Regime, the Wassenaar Club, and the Australia Group, and by conduct that has often been more correct than that of several formal members of these regimes. External Affairs Minister Jaswant Singh told Parliament in 2000 that "India is a nuclear weapon state. Though not a party to the NPT, India's policies have been consistent with the key provisions of the NPT as they apply to nuclear weapon states."[7] He then went on to explain, article by article, how India's behavior was consistent with the obligations of an NWS under the Nuclear Non-Proliferation Treaty.

The broader issue from an Indian point of view is whether existing international nonproliferation regimes and disarmament efforts address our security concerns, and what we should do about that. My sense is that these regimes do not address our most serious security concerns. Some, such as Pakistani proliferation, possible new weapon states in Asia, and the multiple conventional and nonconventional threats to our security, have clearly defeated the international nonproliferation regimes. Nor does existing discourse promise a way forward to nuclear disarmament. But even though the regimes do not address critical Indian concerns, they still have some utility for India. We would be worse off without them, and we have an interest in not opposing them or acting in contravention of their stipulations, as successive Indian governments of various hues have recognized. We also clearly have an interest in improving these regimes, and if possible working out a new paradigm with the other powers that would improve our security. If we do not do so, and if we act as if the global nuclear debate were irrelevant to our situation, we risk being irrelevant to the world's concerns and needlessly throwing away one possible instrument that could conceivably enhance our security.

STRATEGY IN ASIA'S CHANGING SECURITY LANDSCAPE

Such larger strategic questions, of which there are many, are created by the speed with which the situation is changing around us. They merit far more rigorous analysis and considerably more education of public opinion in India. They reflect the influence that technology is having on strategy, and the need for India to build up its own expertise about this interface.

The creation of nuclear weapons by atomic physicists brought into being weapons of such unimaginable power that they changed the way in which war had been thought of over previous centuries. The atomic military revolution required the development of a doctrine and a force capable of using the technology in a new, innovative, and unexpected way. The power of these weapons made war between the superpowers irrational under all but the most extreme circumstances. As Bernard Brodie explained in 1946, conventional military wisdom in the form of the principles of war simply did not apply in the nuclear world. Surprise and concentration of force no longer guaranteed victory: "Thus far the chief purpose of our military establishment has been to win wars. From now on its chief purpose must be to avert them. It can have almost no other useful purpose."[8] The nuclear era was therefore an era of the wars of decolonization or national liberation, of small wars, for the most part involving proxies rather than direct contention between the great powers as was the earlier norm in the wars of the industrial age before 1945.

Deterrence, pinpointed by Brodie as the sole purpose for possessing nuclear weapons, threatens the infliction of unacceptable damage on an enemy that might attempt to win a nuclear exchange. This is paradoxical. To prevent the use of nuclear weapons, the adversary must be convinced of the certainty of their use in a retaliatory strike. The development of deterrence theory, different from earlier versions of dissuasion or coercion, and its ramifications, including game theory and other refinements, was a direct result of the development of nuclear weapons. Since deterrence is sensitive to technological change, it sustained military R&D efforts right through the Cold War.

There are, of course, problems with relying on deterrence. What if some possessor of nuclear weapons did not understand that these weapons were not meant for use or as warfighting weapons? Fortunately, nuclear weapons are the product of big science; they require significant capital investments and large and complex facilities. They were therefore in the hands of states. They have stayed there despite determined efforts by terrorists and others to get their hands on them. As a result, it has been possible to deal with the proliferation of nuclear weapons and their limitation through politics and interstate mechanisms such as the International Atomic Energy Agency (IAEA) and the Nuclear Non-Proliferation Treaty.

Where nuclear weapons placed unimaginable power in the hands of possessor states, the revolution in information and communications technology (ICT) placed power in the hands of small groups and individuals, and made the state's control over its physical borders irrelevant, while creating a whole new domain for contention in cyberspace. The state's legal monopoly of violence, long a fiction in practice, has now been exposed. And the new ICT technologies promote alternative forms of war. By enabling and empowering individual communications and small-group operations, these technologies make guerrilla warfare and subconventional conflict more likely, as also the use of asymmetry and deception, conflict at the lower end of the spectrum of violence, and cyber operations against nuclear weapon programs.

Many habits of thought that we learned in the nuclear age are now being stood on their head as a result of the ICT revolution. When attacks in cyberspace are close to the speed of light, conventional deterrence can barely operate, and there is a clear premium on offense rather than defense. Cyberspace is a borderless, anonymous, and anarchic domain where it is hard to ascribe an origin or source to attacks and other malicious activities.

Nuclear threats are only one, and not necessarily the most urgent, among those that India faces in its unique strategic situation. But the nuclear threat is potentially the most devastating. Indians live in the most heavily nuclearized neighborhood in the world, where nonstate actors are increasingly powerful (and some state actors behave as nonstate actors do); where several powers are rising simultaneously in a crowded environment; and where competition is restrained only by these powers' domestic preoccupations and perceived interests, and not by any institutional structures or memories of the benefits of cooperative behavior. Fortunately, the far-sighted actions that were taken since the 1950s to keep our nuclear options open, to build our capabilities and weaponize them, have enabled us to deal with nuclear threats so far. But things are changing rapidly, and we must understand the shifting capabilities of other powers in Asia and the effect it has on our security.

Indians often seem to assume that India is a status quo power in foreign affairs. This is a big change from how we saw our place in the world until the early 1980s. Thinking of India as a status quo power may have been a useful working hypothesis in the last few decades, so long as we were bent on avoiding external entanglements. But as the external environment is actually deteriorating, we may have to revisit this assumption. I am no longer sure that we are truly a status quoist power, or that we can be one if we wish to maintain the momentum of domestic growth and change.

Going forward, the real dangers of nuclear proliferation elsewhere in the world are less than those from weak political and civilian control over Pakistani nuclear weapons. Using and managing nuclear weapons is a complex task, and one not easily undertaken by terrorist groups.

More likely and more serious is an insider threat, such as a rogue Pakistan Air Force pilot deciding to take the law into his own hands. If the Pakistan Army does actually develop and deploy tactical nuclear weapons, as the leadership wishes India and the world to believe, command and control over the only militarily controlled nuclear weapons program in the world will be even more tenuous than it is today.

For the present, hewing to a no-first-use policy is the best response to the situation India faces. But that situation is changing rapidly, and it is important that India think though the alternatives, continue to master the relevant technologies, and be ready to respond should its nuclear security challenge change in fundamental ways.

India's choices on nuclear weapons, while couched in moral and elevated terms in their expression, have been fundamentally realistic and sober, based on a calculus of security that, to a very great extent, is unique to India. Many of those decisions, by Homi Bhabha, Jawaharlal Nehru, Raja Ramanna, Indira Gandhi, A. B. Vajpayee, Manmohan Singh, and others, were made without fanfare but in the awareness that they were being made for a great power and had to stand the test of time. That India paid a short-term economic price for those decisions in terms of sanctions and technology denial is indisputable. But even Morarji Desai, who came to power as prime minister in 1977 convinced that India should forswear nuclear weapons and sign the Nuclear Non-Proliferation Treaty, soon saw the disadvantages to India of that course of action when other powers, particularly China, would not subject themselves to the same restraints. That was why when President Carter pushed at what he expected to be an open nuclear door with the Gandhian Morarji, Desai pushed back.[9]

Nuclear decisionmaking in India is an example of strategically bold decisions combined with tactically cautious steps, a pattern that is not uniquely Indian but one that Indian foreign and security policy has made its own.

CHAPTER SIX

A Final Word

True power speaks softly. It has no reason to shout.
—Mahatma Gandhi

When the effective leader is finished with his work, the people say
it happened naturally.
—Lao Tse

Colourful and rich is India; loveable and charming is the life of men.
—Buddha at eighty to Ananda, leaving Vaisali
for Kusinagara, where he passed away

WHAT DO THE FIVE instance of policymaking described in this book
tell us about how states behave, and about India's foreign policy
choices?

We have considered the uses of force in Sri Lanka in 2009 and after
the Mumbai attack. Sri Lanka is the only case I know of in which a
terrorist group was completely eliminated by a conventional army. And
we have seen the limited utility of certain kinds of military force in
dealing with state-sponsored, cross-border terrorism in our examination of 26/11. We have also considered whether well-meaning efforts
to bring cease-fires or peace talks might, counterintuitively, increase
the overall cost of wars in terms of human suffering and casualties,

particularly among civilians, as in Sri Lanka's twenty-six-year-long civil war.

We have looked at the dangers that weak or fragile states such as Pakistan and many of those in West Asia pose to their neighbors and peace, and have considered whether induced partitions and artificial boundaries are not major sources of instability.

Equally, we have seen the limits of diplomacy and statecraft, often because the states that make up the international community respond even to horrific developments only on the basis of a narrow calculation of self-interest. We saw this after the Mumbai attack and during the Sri Lankan civil war. The balancing of sometimes contradictory interests that even major powers with direct interests have to undertake, as India had to do in Sri Lanka, limits choices and effective international responses. In most cases governments are forced into mini-max decisions—minimizing the harm and maximizing the benefit to their interests. There are seldom clearly right or wrong answers or evident successes at the time the decisions are made and implemented.

Because force, diplomacy, and even statecraft may be of limited utility in certain situations, and because military force rather than diplomacy or political process prevailed in some of the situations described here, it is logical to ask whether there are times and places when war should be given a chance. In effect, statecraft raises ethical dilemmas. Is waging brutal war justified if it ends the killing and prevents more deaths of innocents? Is killing one person to save five a moral stance? Does the common good override individual morality? These questions are only touched on in this book; there are no clear and final answers.

For me, the examination of choices suggests there is no single correct or right answer to the questions foreign policy throws up, no answers that are valid in all circumstances. Instead, the best a practitioner can do is be aware of and open to the possibilities and consequences of choices, something that historians are trained to do by their discipline. Strategy is, in effect, a practical affair; it is about achieving one's goals with the means available.

The policy discussions in this book represent a practitioner's view, not a theorist's. If these extended essays have left readers with some sense of the complexity and joys of foreign policy decisionmaking, of the balancing of interests that it requires, and of minimizing harm and maximizing gain, in situations where not all considerations are entirely synchronized, then this book has served a purpose.

INDIA'S PREDILECTIONS

In reflecting on the choices made at critical points in the ongoing development of India's foreign policy, it is natural to consider what they may reveal of India's predilections. When India becomes a great power, as I believe it must, it is the nation's predilections that will determine what manner of great power India chooses to be.

The Determinant Role of the Prime Minister—Personality Matters

An overwhelming observation is that personalities matter. None of the choices examined in this book would have been made or sustained were it not for the leaders taking charge and driving change. The Civil Nuclear Initiative with the United States depended on Prime Minister Manmohan Singh's dogged persistence. Prime Minister Narasimha Rao ensured political acceptability in India for the Border Peace and Tranquility Agreement with China. Prime Minister Rajiv Gandhi was central to the Indian intervention in Sri Lanka, in life and in death. It could be argued that foreign and security policies everywhere are the last portion of sovereign decisionmaking that remains primarily the prerogative of the individual leader in all systems of government. Even in the United States, where government has been consciously designed with checks and balances to avoid the accumulation of power in any one branch, foreign policy is one area where the president's personality and the president's choices matter to a much greater degree than in other spheres. In India since Nehru's time, foreign policy has always been directly managed by the prime minister; strong external affairs ministers, such as Pranab Mukherjee, are the exception.

Each of India's prime ministers made—chose to make—significant strategic decisions that had a long-term impact on the future of India: Jawaharlal Nehru and nonalignment, Indira Gandhi and the birth of Bangladesh in 1971, P. V. Narasimha Rao on the Border Peace and Tranquility Agreement and economic reform, Atal Bihari Vajpayee to test nuclear weapons in 1998 and in diplomacy with Pakistan, and Manmohan Singh with the Civil Nuclear Initiative and settling issues with Pakistan. Each of the initiatives or cases examined in this book changed the landscape of, the discourse about, and the benchmarks for Indian foreign policy. If the 123 Agreement raised expectations of India-U.S. relations to an impossibly high pitch, the 26/11 attack on Mumbai dropped expectations of Pakistan so low as to limit future policy choices.

In each of these cases the easy choice would have been to carry on as before, letting sleeping dogs lie, rather than embarking on uncharted initiatives with countries like the United States, China, Pakistan, and Sri Lanka, all of which had earlier proved to be difficult partners. But changes in the international situation, in those countries, and in India's own condition and capabilities called for changed Indian responses. And in each of these cases the Indian leadership took the strategically bold decisions needed to change course.

Boldness in Policy Conception, Caution in Implementation

These policy decisions were strategically bold but tactically cautious. There are some who argue that there is "a unique Indian strategic culture of restraint."[1] For instance, India chose to regard nuclear weapons as primarily political tools and not as warfighting weapons. This is described by R. M. Basrur as the political symbolism of nuclear weapons overriding any prospective military use.[2] To my mind this is to be blinded by tactical caution to strategic boldness of conception. After all, how many states that retained their nuclear weapons option by not signing the Nuclear Non-Proliferation Treaty immediately after it was agreed to in 1967 stayed the course and actually exercised their option without breaking their word? Other than India, not one.

In each instance that we have examined there was considerable audacity in the conception and in decisions relating to the choice. Whether it was the decision to adopt no first use of nuclear weapons as official doctrine, or to legalize the status quo on the Chinese border, or to enter into the Civil Nuclear Initiative with the United States, it took courage and foresight to make the necessary decisions. At the same time, there was marked caution in their implementation and working out. What we have seen is boldness in conception allied with caution in implementation. Therefore, to my mind, to speak only of a unique Indian culture of restraint would not be accurate or complete.

This caution in practice may owe to systemic factors: since foreign policy decisionmaking is so centralized in the prime minister, and the Ministry of External Affairs lacks capability in India, no single actor or hierarchy in India is sufficiently empowered or has the time to ensure that policy is implemented satisfactorily. The corollary to the central role of the prime minister in decisionmaking is weak institutionalization of foreign policy implementation in India. Weak institutionalization is reflected in weak policy implementation. India has serious capacity issues in the implementation of foreign policy and lacks the institutional depth to see policy through.

In my experience the structured and formal process of decisionmaking in India is invariably preceded by considerable informal consultation and discussion centered on the prime minister. Before formal decisions were taken by the Cabinet Committee on Security, they were invariably thoroughly discussed and considered beforehand. This results in slow but sure decisionmaking—not as decisive or as attractive a form of leadership as charisma demands, but certainly more likely to result in a better decision than any one person's preferences. It has been the ability of leaders like Narasimha Rao, A. B. Vajpayee, and Manmohan Singh to know how to lead and manage this process, democratic inside but opaque to the outside world, and to intervene at the right moment that has achieved outcomes from an institutionally challenged apparat.

The best that can be said is that the institutionalization of foreign and security policymaking in India has been weak, and is only now beginning with the creation of the National Security Council and the Nuclear Command Authority a little over a decade ago. The role and effectiveness of the Cabinet Committee on Security and its predecessor, the Cabinet Committee on Political Affairs, have varied considerably from government to government and are less today than in Manmohan Singh's much more collegial government. In foreign policy, policymaking has always been almost entirely within the individual domain of the prime minister, a practice begun by Nehru and carried on by all his successors. The result is that grand strategy, the conception of India's place and role in the world, has been bold, innovative, and shared across political parties in the spectrum. It is uncertain whether Prime Minister Narendra Modi will continue this tradition as he has yet to spell out a vision or strategy. The current NDA government is open to a charge of strategic incoherence, of having a vision deficit, and of forwarding a policy marked by much activity and energetic projection without an overarching conceptual framework. Carrying on previous governments' policies may be sufficient to deal pragmatically with an incoherent world but is already running up against others' strategies and new and inconvenient realities.

Realism in Policymaking

The other standout feature of the policymaking instances discussed in this book is the realistic basis on which the choices were made. Thirty years after traumatic defeat in the 1962 border war with China, India was willing to accept reality on the border and formalize it in the Border Peace and Tranquility Agreement in 1993. The choices were realistic despite the normative and moral terms in which India chooses to present its policies—describing the Nuclear Non-Proliferation Treaty as discriminatory, or using equity and moral criteria to explain its choices on hard interests such as trade and climate change and energy issues. In practice, India has been quick to react to changes in the objective situation. The end of the bipolar world in which the United States and the Soviet Union stood alone as superpowers and the collapse of the Soviet Union occasioned India's outreach to the United States, India's economic liberalization, and the opening to China in Rajiv Gandhi's visit and the Border Peace and Tranquility Agreement. The end of the United States' moment as the sole superpower, which came after the 2008 global financial crisis, and the rise of China led India to enter into a strategic partnership with the United States whose potent symbol was the civil nuclear initiative, to the Look East policy, and to other internal and external balancing steps. Prime Minister Modi doubled down on that bet on the United States by inviting President Obama to India's Republic Day in January 2015 and declaring a joint strategic vision for the Asia-Pacific region.

Process

The function of the domestic political process in Indian foreign policy seems to be unique. All legal and constitutional power to conduct foreign relations, declare war, and sign and ratify treaties is with the Executive. Of course, government is dependent on its control of the lower House of Parliament for its existence. But as the Civil Nuclear Initiative showed, even when for extended periods it appeared that a majority in the House opposed a policy, the government was able to move forward and implement it steadily. The final vote of no confidence was won by members voting politically rather than on the merits or according to their convictions about the advantages of the initiative. Working with Sri Lanka in 2009 involved the relationship between internal politics in Sri Lanka and in India and how they constrained and almost determined the choices available. We also saw in Sri Lanka that there is no external fix for a broken internal political system. And the Border Peace and Tranquility Agreement with China was made possible by Prime Minister Rao's skillful management of the domestic political process to ensure the smooth pursuit of foreign policy goals.

"Escaping Forward"

India's leaders have also used crises to *"fuite en avant"* (or "escape forward," as the French say), as clever elites have done through history, seeing troubles as opportunities to change policies and propel gains that are politically difficult to achieve in normal times. The border agreement with China was an innovation prompted by the end of the Cold War, as was the wave of reform, which itself was set off by the Indian economic crisis of 1991. The civil nuclear initiative with the United States was a response to sanctions and international prohibitions and condemnation of India's 1998 nuclear weapon tests. The question is not just whether policy is reactive or proactive but how one reacts to the crises and events that inevitably will arise and put paid to the best laid plans.

AN INDIAN WAY?

Do these predilections of Indian foreign policy amount to a strategic culture that is uniquely Indian?

The idea that the strategic behavior of nations has cultural roots has become increasingly popular in recent years. In some ways this is self-evident, and the kernel of the idea is old. Sun Tzu says, "Know your enemy and yourself and you will be undefeated in battle." All significant traditions incorporate a variant of this idea. But the concept that nations have a unique strategic culture of their own that determines their choices is relatively new. Historically, the rediscovery of culture is a response to crisis, as it is today. For instance, immediately after the shock of 1857 the British produced a series of handbooks to explain "the natives." The Cold War and the fear of nuclear apocalypse gave a new impetus to understanding the adversary's strategic culture. The nuclear strategist Bernard Brodie said that "good strategy presumes good anthropology and sociology."[3] And today, when the United States and other powers struggle to convert overwhelming conventional and tactical battlefield supremacy into lasting political triumph and outcomes against both state and nonstate actors in the Middle East and Afghanistan, explanations are again sought in cultural factors and strategic culture. Defense Secretary Robert Gates asked about Osama bin Laden, "How has one man in a cave managed to out-communicate the world's greatest communications society?"

It is a small step from these observations to argue that national and organizational strategies are culturally determined, generated by long-term evolution, history, geography, and experience. In essence, the "culturalists" argue that ideational factors are better explanations than realist factors such as objective interests and the material balance of power. To an extent, the concept was useful: it moved thinking away from the realist assumption that "strategic man" is acultural, rational, and universal, the same across nations and civilizations, responding to stimuli and incentives in the same way. This is clearly not the case in reality.

The trouble with the concept of strategic culture is that it seems to privilege cultural explanations for state behavior and thereby to add a deterministic element to an analysis of foreign and security policies. What people say and declare, or how they present and perceive themselves, is not always how they behave, as we all know from experience. The truth is surely somewhere in between these two extremes. Culture itself changes and evolves; while it exerts an influence and is a factor, it is not the determinant of strategic behavior.

There is an ongoing debate in the literature as to whether India has a strategic culture or not. In the early 1990s George Tanham of the Rand Corporation argued in comments often echoed by Indian commentators that India lacks a strategic culture.[4] On the other hand, Rodney Jones has argued otherwise—that India's strategic culture is "more distinct and coherent than that of most contemporary nation states."[5] Others, such as Waheguru Sidhu, for instance, have written on the ancient roots of Indian strategy.[6] There is an increasing body of literature by younger scholars looking for Indian and non-Western sources of Indian foreign policy and security ideas and conduct.[7]

My own sense is that there is indeed an Indian way of doing things, of conducting foreign policy. But it is not clear to me whether it can be said to amount to a strategic culture, which in any case also evolves in the normal historical process. There are risks with concepts like strategic culture that make them useful but not binding on us. Taken too far, they can amount to a form of cultural determinism, almost of Orientalism, in our case, as they suggest that foreign policy and strategic choices are predetermined by cultural factors. This is clearly not always true. Nor is it sufficient to explain what we see around us. At the other extreme, cultural relativism or pure realism assumes that all states are rational actors that behave similarly in the same circumstances and pursue identical interests. This is also clearly not true.

Defining the Indian way in foreign policy is difficult, just as it is hard to put into words what makes a person Indian, since we base our nationhood not on religion, ethnicity, language, or any of the standard nineteenth-century criteria but on an idea of India. However, though hard to define, the world knows an Indian, an Indian diplomat, and Indian foreign policy when it sees them. If there is an Indian way in foreign policy, it is marked by a combination of boldness in conception and caution in implementation, by the dominant and determining role of the prime minister, by a didactic negotiating style, by a fundamentally realistic approach masked by normative rhetoric, by comfort in a plural and diverse world or multiverse, and, most consistently, by a consciousness of India's destiny as a great power.

ALL IN ALL, the result of these and similar choices by India has been its steady accumulation of power and independent agency in the international system into which India is increasingly integrated. Cumulatively, India still has to learn how to deal with Pakistan, with all its discontents, and it has seen its China policy veer from failure to success to needing readjustment again. India has a mixed record of dealing with a transactional United States, even as it has met reasonable goals in its relationships with other neighbors and major powers such as Japan, Russia, and the rest of the Asia-Pacific region. But as India's integration into the international system grows, it will become even more important that India continue to make the right foreign and security policy choices in terms of maximizing gains and minimizing losses. Initiative and risk taking must be strategic, not tactical, at India's present level of power, to avoid the fate of powers in history whose rise was thwarted.

During the period of the choices considered in this book, India shifted strategic focus from Pakistan to China, fully operationalized its nuclear weapons program and deterrence capabilities, accumulated economic power at an unprecedented rate, with GDP growth rates unmatched in past decades, strengthened its military posture along the borders, and created new national security structures. The verdict on this period's work will come when India finds it needs to turn to its economic sinews to support and sustain its military and political quest as a great power.

India's influence is considerable in the immediate neighborhood. As a result of the nation's economic growth, India is listened to with respect and consulted in global economic councils. The new role of the G-20 is tribute to the shift in global economic power and interdependence. But political and military power is the core, and something that existing power holders do not share voluntarily or easily. On the larger political issues of the day India is consulted and has views that matter.

India's independence of action (or independent agency) has grown over time. In 1948, India went to the UN seeking help against Pakistani aggression in Jammu and Kashmir. In 1971, India helped the people of Bangladesh create their own state, using force in self-defense and in the service of a clear and legitimate political goal. And in 2008, helped by the United States and other major powers, the international community rewrote the rules for nuclear cooperation with India, making an exception in its favor in the Nuclear Suppliers Group. That is progress.

INDIA'S FUTURE STRATEGIC CHOICES should not be difficult to predict. The overriding consideration in all the policy choices examined in this book was the goal of transforming India, and that is unlikely to change for some time to come, since the task itself is so great. Choices will be ranked in importance in terms of how they promote that goal, and how they affect its achievement. But the complexity of the tactical choices that even a clear strategic goal throws up suggests that at this level, India's course is much less predictable. For instance, after the 26/11 Mumbai attacks, the then government of India decided not to respond with overt military force. But future governments are unlikely to respond similarly if faced with a similar attack. Deterring the state sponsors of terrorism requires some unpredictability of response and a conviction in the minds of terrorists and their state sponsors that retaliation will occur. The government of India has signaled its preparedness to respond militarily through statements and demonstrations of intent since 26/11. The Pakistan Army and Pakistani jihadis, for their part, have tested the government of India's tolerance by gradually raising the level of lethality and the complexity of cross-border terrorist attacks since 2014. If deterrence fails and there is another major attack, the government of India will have a strong motive to reinforce fear in the minds of the state sponsors of cross-border terrorism in Pakistan by responding with force.

There is no question that the context in which India will make its future choices is getting more complex with the rise of China, the ineffectiveness of existing institutions of global governance, the continuing world economic crisis since 2008, the pervasive sense of insecurity in the Asia-Pacific region, evident in the arms race under way in the region, and in the contested global commons in cyberspace, outer space, and the seas near China.

Even so, as uncertainty grows in the international system, India's capacity is also growing. Barring a fundamental reordering or turmoil in the world order (which, rightly or wrongly, each generation believes it is witness to), the Indian predilections mentioned here should continue to hold. India will continue to seek to enlarge its strategic autonomy, remain fiercely independent, and remain convinced of its exceptional status and interests in the international system. This almost guarantees that other powers will react to India's selective engagement and strategic autonomy by accusing the country of free-loading. But so long as India remains unique in its location at the junction of the world's major energy and trade routes, in its internal economic and social structure, and in its strong cultural identity, Indian foreign policy exceptionalism will continue to serve India's specific interests. The institutional and other weaknesses and domestic preoccupations mentioned here will inhibit India's becoming an expeditionary power and lead the country to rely more on diplomatic means than military force to get its way and, increasingly, to shape the external environment. If individuals attempt to go against the grain of policy as implemented so far, objective reality and India's condition are likely to bring them up short, painfully.

I am convinced that India will be a great power if it continues on its present course. This will not be through the exercise of soft power. I have never heard anyone responsible saying so or professing this particular belief. Nor will it come about by others giving great power status to India through some mysterious process of entitlement or accretion. Nor will it happen through a variant of nineteenth-century European power politics, which, despite all that we hear from scholars, was a much simpler task than that facing Indian policymakers. (Bismarck had to deal with one continental system, which by its nature was a zero-sum game. India has to deal with a complex continental system, the rise of China, and simultaneously with an equally complex maritime system, which is a positive-sum game.) Instead, I believe that India will be a great power by building its own strength and capabilities and continuing to show wisdom, realism, and good sense in its choice of engagements abroad. As an old-fashioned patriot, I am confident that ultimately the Indian people, history, and geography will prevail, as they always have.

I do believe that "speak softly and carry a big stick" is likely to be a more productive policy for India to mobilize in dealing with the consequences of China's rise and the other changes we see around us. Like China itself, and every other successful rising power in history, India too should follow a variant of Deng's Twenty-Four-Character strategy,[8] or of the policies expounded in George Washington's farewell address, a Bismarckian policy rather than the vainglorious temptations that led Kaiser Wilhelm II astray. As Bhishma said in his advice to kings while dying on his bed of arrows, "He who is silent secures the following of others; the restrained one enjoys everything in life."[9]

Why am I sure that India will be a great power, despite all the limitations and frustrations that Indians express so vocally, eloquently, and often?[10] Because it is in India's interest to be a great power. This is one goal that all Indians share irrespective of the shade of their politics. Besides, to transform India we need to create an enabling external environment if we are to develop a natural resource–poor India rich in human capital. The issue is not whether India will be a great power. It is a great power in certain respects. Consider the geopolitical importance of India—a country home to one-sixth of humanity, nurturing a large and fast-growing economy, situated in a vital spot on multiple political fault lines, with a great civilization—such a country is bound to be a great power. The issue is how India chooses to exercise the power that it is accumulating and already possesses.

THE PURPOSE OF POWER

And this brings us to the purpose of power. Why should India want to be a great power? Theoretically it could be argued that, like postwar Japan until recently, or Australia and Canada, Indians should be satisfied with concentrating on our own economic development and should leave it to others to provide for our security. India cannot accept that, for a simple reason. India cannot rely on others for its security because its economic, political, and security interests are unique, a function of its unique history, geography, and culture. If we wish to abolish mass poverty, hunger, illiteracy, and disease and modernize our country—or, as Gandhiji said so much more elegantly, "wipe the tear from the eye of every Indian"—we can do so only by becoming a great power, with the ability to shape the international system and environment to our purposes. India is in a unique position, and no one else will solve its problems. It therefore seeks and obtains special solutions, as in the nuclear nonproliferation regime through the Civil Nuclear Cooperation Initiative, the Border Peace and Tranquility Agreement with China, and other international agreements. Strategic autonomy is not just a slogan or a desire but a necessity if we are to transform India. India is and has been an anti-status-quo power, seeking to revise and reform the international order since Nehru's day. That we have not succeeded so far is evident. Also evident is that we have sought to do so by working within the existing order, not by overthrowing it but by improving it to accommodate India's interests.

That India needs to be a great power if we want to have a chance of succeeding is also apparent. India's transformation requires engagement with the world, enhancing security in its neighborhood; contributing within its capacity to global public goods such as the freedom of the seas; and shaping outcomes on crucial issues such as energy security and climate change.

For a considerable time to come, India will be a significant power with many poor people. We must always therefore be conscious of the difference between weight, influence, and power. Power is the ability to create and sustain outcomes. Weight we have, our influence is growing, but our power remains to grow and should first be used for our domestic transformation.

History is replete with examples of rising powers that prematurely thought their time had come, that mistook influence and weight for real power. Their rise, like that of Wilhelmine Germany or militarist Japan, was cut short prematurely.

At the risk of disappointing those who call on India to be a "responsible" power—meaning they want us to do what they wish—and at the risk of disappointing Indians who like to dream of India as an old-fashioned superpower, I would only say, as Indira Gandhi once said, "India will be a different power" and will continue to walk its own path in the world. That is the only responsible way for us.

So we end with more questions and possibilities than we began, as all good quests should. Except that the better we know our past, the better prepared we are for our future.

Men are apt to think in great crises that when all has been done they still have something left to do, and when all has been said that they have still not said enough.
      —THUCYDIDES, ca. 400 BCE

Notes

INTRODUCTION

1. Jonathan Power, "Talking to the New Prime Minister of India," *New York Times*, May 24, 2004.

2. Chanakya, the third-century BCE author of the *Arthashastra*, on statecraft, was reputedly the tutor of India's first unifier, Chandragupta Maurya. The term "Chanakyan" is used in India as "Machiavellian" is in Europe, both somewhat unfairly.

CHAPTER 1

1. Details are available in the *Report of the Officials of the Governments of India and the People's Republic of China on the Boundary Question* (Government of India, Ministry of External Affairs, February 1961), published by the Government of India after talks with the Chinese in 1960–61.

2. See Matthew W. Mosca, *From Frontier Policy to Foreign Policy: The Question of India and the Transformation of Geopolitics in Qing China* (Stanford University Press, 2013).

3. Prime Minister Nehru to Premier Zhou Enlai, letter of December 14, 1958, in "Notes, Memoranda and Letters Exchanged and Agreements signed between the Governments of India and China," White Papers, vol. I (1954 to August 1959) (Government of India, Ministry of External Affairs), p. 48.

4. Premier Zhou Enlai to Prime Minister Nehru, letter of January 23, 1959, in "Notes, Memoranda and Letters Exchanged and Agreements signed between the Governments of India and China," White Papers, vol. I, p. 52.

5. See "Notes, Memoranda and Letters Exchanged and Agreements signed between the Governments of India and China," White Papers, vols. I and II

(1954 to November 1959) (Government of India, Ministry of External Affairs, 1959 and 1960).

6. Prime Minister Jawahrlal Nehu, letter to Premier Chou Enlai, letter of October 27, 1962, in "Notes, Memoranda and Letters Exchanged and Agreements signed between the Governments of India and China," White Papers, vol. VIII (October 1962 to January 1963), p. 6.

7. Premier Chou En-lai to the Prime Minister of India, letter of November 4, 1962, in "Notes, Memoranda and Letters Exchanged and Agreements signed between the Governments of India and China," White Papers, vol. VIII (October 1962 to January 1963), p. 7.

8. See Gyalo Thondup and Anne F. Thurston, *The Noodle Maker of Kalimpong* (New York: Public Affairs, 2015), for an account by the Dalai Lama's brother of these events.

9. This was the origin of the semantic debate right through the officials' talks in the 1980s about "mutual understanding and mutual accommodation," language proposed by the Chinese, and "mutual understanding and mutual adjustment," language insisted on by the Indians.

10. Its formal name is the Agreement Between the Government of the Republic of India and the Government of the People's Republic of China on Confidence-Building Measures in the Military Field Along the Line of Actual Control in the India-China Border Areas, signed November 29, 1996.

11. By way of comparison, Israel spends around 6 percent, Saudi Arabia 8–9 percent, Pakistan 4 percent, and the United States 4.6 falling to 3.8 percent of GDP on defense, according to the Word Bank (http://data.worldbank.org /indicator/MS.MIL.XPND.GD.ZS).

12. Mao was referring to the eighteenth-century punitive expedition into Nepal from Tibet by the Qing dynasty and the brief eighth-century Tang dynasty intervention in local disputes in the Nepalese Terai or sub-Himalayan region. See Mosca, *From Frontier Policy to Foreign Policy*.

CHAPTER 2

1. The Zangger Committee was formed in 1971 by fifteen nuclear supplier states to informally agree which supplies should trigger the application of safeguards. India's nuclear test of 1974 led to such arrangements being formalized and made legally binding by the Nuclear Suppliers Group, which first met in November 1975.

2. The Nuclear Non-Proliferation Treaty of 1967 had divided the world into nuclear weapon states (NWS) and non-nuclear weapon states (NNWS). The latter abjured the use of nuclear weapons and were under IAEA safeguards involving inspections and checks to ensure their compliance. The former promised only to make a good faith effort to negotiate nuclear disarmament and were not obliged to accept safeguards on their nuclear programs.

3. The Fissile Material Cut-off Treaty is a proposed treaty to prohibit the further production of fissile material for nuclear weapons. Its terms and language remain to be drafted, negotiated, and agreed upon.

4. Section 123 of the U.S. Atomic Energy Act of 1954, "Cooperation with Other Nations," requires "a specific agreement for significant transfers of nuclear material, equipment, or components from the United States to another nation." Countries wishing to enter into such arrangements with the United States must agree to the U.S.-mandated nuclear nonproliferation norms. See the website of the National Nuclear Security Administration (nnsa.energy.gov).

5. The April 2005 Agreement on the Political Parameters and Guiding Principles for the Settlement of the Boundary Question, signed by India and China when Chinese premier Wen Jiabao visited New Delhi, suggested that a boundary settlement with China might be possible.

6. Condoleezza Rice, "Campaign 2000: Promoting the National Interest," *Foreign Affairs*, January/February 2000.

7. U.S. Department of State, *The National Security Strategy of the United States of America,* the White House, September 17, 2002 (http://www.state.gov /documents/organization/63562.pdf).

8. The Missile Technology Control Regime was established in 1987 and seeks to curb the spread of unmanned delivery systems for nuclear weapons that carry a minimum payload of 500 kg a minimum distance of 300 kilometers. Thirty-four countries are members of the MTCR. India has adhered to its terms and sought membership.

9. The formal name of the act is the Weapons of Mass Destruction and Their Delivery Systems (Prohibition of Unlawful Activities) Act of 2005. Unsurprisingly, it is normally called the WMD Act.

10. The July 18, 2005, Joint Statement had committed both countries to "enable full civil nuclear energy co-operation and trade," and this had been one of the major arguments for the initiative in India.

11. The IAEA Additional Protocol is a legal document that gives the IAEA certain expanded access to information and sites not originally envisaged in safeguards agreements entered into by states with the IAEA before 1997. As of March 2016, 128 Additional Protocols are in force with 127 states and Euratom.

CHAPTER 3

1. Lydia Polgreen and Vikas Bajaj, "Suspect Stirs Mumbai Court by Confessing," *New York Times*, July 20, 2009.

2. Indo-Asian News Service (IANS), "India Says All Options Open, Wants Pakistan to Act," *New Indian Express*, December 2, 2008 (http://www .newindianexpress.com/nation/article11087.ece). See also "All Options Open, Pranab Warns Pak," *India Today*, December 22, 2008 (http://indiatoday.intoday .in/).

3. See Maj. Gen. (Retd.) Muhammad Akbar Khan, *Raiders in Kashmir* (Lahore: Jang Publishers, 1992). Khan was the Pakistan Army officer who organized the "tribal raiders."

4. See, for instance, David Sanger and others, "In 2008 Mumbai Attacks, Piles of Spy Data, but an Uncompleted Puzzle," *New York Times,* December 21,

2014, about what the United States and others knew before the attack (http://www.nytimes.com/2014/12/22/world/asia/in-2008-mumbai-attacks-piles-of-spy-data-but-an-uncompleted-puzzle.html). See also Sebastian Rotella, "Did the US Know More Than It Let On about Mumbai Attacks Suspect?," PBS and ProPublica, November 22, 2011 (http://www.pbs.org/wgbh/pages/frontline/afghanistan-pakistan/davis-headley/did-the-us-know-more-than-it-let-on-about-mumbai-attacks-suspect/). For several conspiracy theories about Headley and others, see Cathy Scott-Clerk and Adrian Levy, *The Siege: The Attack on the Taj* (New York: Penguin, 2013).

5. Efraim Inbar and Eitan Shamir, " 'Mowing the Grass': Israel's Strategy for Protracted Intractable Conflict," *Journal of Strategic Studies* 37, no. 1 (2013), pp. 67–90. In a separate reprint, the quotations are found on pp. 4, 1, and 6.

6. Thomas Schelling, *The Strategy of Conflict* (Harvard University Press, 1960), p. 9.

7. See the statement by Prime Minister Manmohan Singh's special envoy, Satinder K. Lambah, at a seminar at Srinagar University, May 13, 2014, on the Indian Ministry of External Affairs website (mea.gov.in); Steve Coll, "The Back Channel, India and Pakistan's Secret Kashmir Talks," *The New Yorker*, March 2, 2009, pp. 38ff. (http://www.newyorker.com/magazine/2009/03/02/the-back-channel); and Khurshid Kasuri, *Neither a Hawk Nor a Dove* (Oxford University Press, 2015).

8. Mark Sykes and François Georges-Picot were British and French diplomats whose secret agreement of 1916 determined post–World War I boundaries between states in the Middle East and sowed the seeds of the Palestinian problem. Sir Cyril Radcliffe was the English lawyer who drew the boundaries between India and Pakistan in five weeks in 1947. Those five weeks were his only acquaintance with the Indian subcontinent and resulted in the boundaries being drawn in haste, secrecy, and ignorance, thus adding to the trauma of Partition.

CHAPTER 4

1. The term *Eelam*, or homeland, had been used by Tamil separatists in India from the early twentieth century, and was probably chosen by the Sri Lankan Tamils to evoke support and sympathy from the much larger Tamil-speaking community in Tamilnadu in India.

2. Ironically, tigers are not native to Sri Lanka, and there are no tigers in nature in Sri Lanka.

3. There may be a parallel worth examining here between the fates of two minorities under British rule in South Asia, namely, the Indian Muslim and the Sri Lankan Tamil. Both were minorities favored by the British administration, were led by small elites, and were used to thinking of themselves as rulers. Among the Sri Lankan Tamils the benefits of education and economic advancement were distributed through the community, but this was not so among the Muslims of India, who were left by the British to the tender devices of their community

leaders. Ultimately some leaders of the Indian Muslims got themselves a separate state in the name of their community but little else; the Sri Lankan Tamils got neither a state of their own nor anything else.

4. A plethora of such groups existed in the 1980s in Sri Lanka, all committed to violence to bring about Tamil Eelam. Some of the more significant ones were:

> EPRLF—Eelam People's Revolutionary Liberation Front. Its leader was K. Pathmanabha.
> EPDP—Eelam People's Democratic Party. Its leader is Douglas Devananda, a former member of EPRLF who left to form EPDP.
> TELO—Tamil Eelam Liberation Organization, once decimated by the LTTE. Its leaders were Kutimani (nickname) and Sri Sabaratnam.
> PLOTE—People's Liberation Organization of Tamil Eelam. Its leader was Uma Maheswaran.
> ENDLF—Eelam National Democratic Liberation Front. Its leader was Paranthan Rajan.
> EROS—Eelam Revolutionary Organization of Students. Its leader was V. Balakumar.
> TMVP—an LTTE splinter group.
> NTT—New Tamil Tigers (Puthiya Thamil Pulikal) (1972–76), predecessor to the LTTE.
> TLO—Tamil Liberation Organization (1974–78).

5. The best account of these events from an Indian point of view by one of the significant participants is still J. N. Dixit, *Assignment Colombo* (Delhi: Konark Publishers, 1998). Dixit was India's high commissioner to Sri Lanka during this period.

6. The JVP, or Janatha Vimukthi Peramuna, founded in the late 1960s by the radical Marxist Rohana Wijeweera, had risen in revolt in 1971, been suppressed, and carried out a campaign of subversion and terrorism in southern Sri Lanka, relying on Sinhala support, from 1987 to 1989. Initially Marxist, in its second incarnation it was increasingly an extreme right Sinhala chauvinist organization.

7. There has been much speculation about Karuna and his motives—whether this was a false flag operation or not. Such speculation was fueled by the fact that he went on to a political career in the province after defecting from the LTTE.

8. Kumaran Pathmanathan, or KP, was the main LTTE arms procurer and money launderer outside Sri Lanka for much of the war. He went by as many as twenty-three aliases but was born Shanmugam Kumaran Tharmalingam. He too was subsequently freed by the Sri Lankan government in October 2012, like other LTTE leaders whose loyalties are now in question. He is still on Interpol's Most Wanted list and is wanted by the Indian authorities for his role in the killing of Rajiv Gandhi and for arms-trafficking offenses.

9. C. A. Chandraprema, *Gota's War: The Crushing of Tamil Tiger Terrorism in Sri Lanka* (Colombo: Piyasiri Printing Systems, 2012).

10. Edward Luttwak, "Give War a Chance," *Foreign Affairs* 78, no. 4 (July/August 1999) (www.foreignaffairs.com/articles/1999-07-01/give-war-chance).

11. Reinhold Niebuhr, *The Irony of American History* (Scribner, 1952).

12. Hannah Arendt, *The Origins of Totalitarianism* (New York: Schocken Books, 1951).

CHAPTER 5

1. The doctrine was unveiled in stages: first as a draft report of the National Security Advisory Board on August 17, 1999 (http://mea.gov.in/in-focus-article .htm?18916/Draft+Report+of+National+Security+Advisory+Board+on+Indian +Nuclear+Doctrine) and thereafter in a press release by the Prime Minister's Office, "Cabinet Committee on Security Reviews Progress in Operationalizing India's Nuclear Doctrine," January 4, 2003 (http://pib.nic.in/archieve/lreleng /lyr2003/rjan2003/04012003/r040120033.html). The text quotations here are from paragraphs 2.4 and 2.5 of the NSAB draft report of August 17, 1999.

2. These red lines were made known to the International Institute for Strategic Studies by Pakistani nuclear command authority officials in late 2001. See, for instance, the transcript of Gen. Khalid Kidwai's conversation with Peter Lavoy at the Carnegie Endowment for International Peace, March 23, 2015 (http://carnegieendowment.org/files/03-230315carnegieKIDWAI.pdf).

3. The situation of separate strategic forces commands for Pakistan's air force and navy is unlike the situation obtaining in India, where the Strategic Forces Command is a joint, interservices command that is staffed by all three services and reports to the Chairman of the Chiefs of Staff Committee and to the Nuclear Command Authority. This reporting structure keeps a civilian finger on the nuclear trigger at all times and unifies command and control.

4. For similar views expressed in public by two former Pakistani foreign secretaries and one air chief, see Agha Shahi, Abdul Sattar, and Air Chief Marshal Zulfikar Ali Khan, "Keeping the Nuclear Peace," *The News International,* October 5, 1999, which argues that Pakistan's nuclear capability deterred India from attacking Pakistan in 1984, 1987, and 1990. See also the transcript of K. Subrahmanyam's 19th Kelkar Alumni Lecture at the Indian Institute of Technology, Kanpur, "India's Nuclear Doctrine," January 22, 2000, countering this claim (http://www.iitkalumni.org/lectures/kelkar/19kelkarlecture.htm).

5. See also the transcript of Gen. Kidwai's conversation with Peter Lavoy, March 23, 2015.

6. The Rawalpindi Conspiracy was an attempted coup d'état against the government of Liaqat Ali Khan, the first prime minister of Pakistan, in 1950. The coup was planned by Maj. Gen. Akbar Khan, a senior commander in the Pakistan Army, who had organized the tribal raiders' attack on Kashmir in 1948.

7. Suo Moto Statement in Parliament on the Sixth Non-Proliferation Treaty Review Conference, May 9, 2000 (http://fas.org/news/india/2000/eam-9may .htm).

8. Bernard Brodie, "Implications for Military Policy," in *The Absolute Weapon: Atomic Power and World Order,* edited by Bernard Brodie (New York: Harcourt, Brace and Co., 1946), p. 74. Brodie himself moved to a virtual rejection of a first-strike strategy in *Strategy in the Missile Age* (Princeton University Press, 1959), arguing for second-strike capabilities targeting military installations, not civilians.

9. See, for example, Jagat S. Mehta, *The Tryst Betrayed: Reflections in Diplomacy and Development* (Delhi: Penguin India, 2014), for an eyewitness account.

CHAPTER 6

1. Kampani, Gaurav, etc., "Secrecy, Civil-Military Relations, and India's Nuclear Weapon Program," *International Security* 39, no. 3 (Winter 2014–15), pp. 202–14.

2. R. M. Basrur, "Nuclear Weapons and India's Strategic Culture," *Journal of Peace Research* 48, no 2 (March 2001).

3. Bernard Brodie, *War and Politics* (New York, 1973), p. 332.

4. George Tanham, "Indian Strategic Thought: An Interpretive Essay," Rand publication, 1992 (http://www.rand.org/content/dam/rand/pubs/reports/2007/R4207.pdf). Also reprinted in *Lancer's Indian Defence Review*, April 1992.

5. Rodney W. Jones, "India's Strategic Culture" (Defense Threat Reduction Agency, Advanced Systems and Concepts Office, October 30, 2006), p. 1 (https://fas.org/irp/agency/dod/dtra/india.pdf).

6. W. P. S. Sidhu, "Of Oral Traditions and Ethnocentric Judgements," in *Securing India: Strategic Thought and Practice,* edited by G. K. Tanham, K. P. Bajpai, and A. Mattoo (Manohar Publications, Delhi, 1996).

7. See Deep Dutta Ray, *The Making of Indian Diplomacy* (Oxford University Press, 2015); Jayashree Vivekanandan, *Interrogating International Relations* (New York: Routledge, 2011); and Arvind Gupta, P. K. Gautam, and others, eds., *Indigenous Historical Knowledge; Kautilya and His Vocabulary,* vols. 1 and 2 (Delhi: IDSA and Pentagon Press, 2015 and 2016).

8. Deng Xiaoping's "twenty-four character" strategy, enunciated in 1992, are "Observe calmly; secure our position; cope with affairs calmly; hide our capacities and bide our time; be good at maintaining a low profile; and never claim leadership" (translation by author).

9. Anushasana Parva, *Mahabharata*, translated by Kisari Mohan Ganguli, book 13.7. (Munshiram Manoharlal Publishers, New Delhi, 2000).

10. See, for instance, Ramachandra Guha, "Will India Become a Superpower?" *Outlook India* 2, June 30, 2008 (http://www.outlookindia.com/magazine/story/will-india-become-a-superpower/237762); and Bharat Karnad, *Why India Is Not a Great Power (Yet)* (Oxford, 2015).

Index

Abu Hamza/Abu Jundal
(aka Zaibuddin Ansari), 65
Ackerman, Gary, 55
Afghanistan: improvements in, 74;
India-Pakistan relations, influence
on, 77; Pakistani actions against,
73–74; U.S. and, 38, 69
Agreement on Military Confidence-
Building Measures (1996), 19, 20
Agreement on the Maintenance of
Peace and Tranquility along the
Line of Actual Control in the
India-China Border Areas (Border
Peace and Tranquility Agreement,
1993): impact of, 20–21; lessons of,
29–33, 126, 129; on mutual and
equal security, 25; negotiations on,
18–19; Rao's skill in achieving,
130; signing of, 19–20. *See also*
Line of Actual Control
Agreement on Trade and Intercourse
(1954), 11
Aksai Chin, territorial dispute over,
11–12, 16
All India Anna Dravida Munnetra
Kazhagam (AIADMK) party, 95
Al Qaeda, 38, 63, 67, 73–74, 80
Anandapuram, Battle of (2009), 97
Anglo-Tibetan Convention (1904), 8, 11

Ansari, Zaibuddin (aka Abu Hamza,
aka Abu Jundal), 65
Arendt, Hannah, 103
Argentina, role in NSG negotiations,
51
Arms race, U.S.-Soviet, 27
"Army of the Righteous." *See*
Lashkar-e-Taiba
Aron, Raymond, 34
Artificial and weak states, 80, 125
Arunachal Pradesh: airfields in, 24;
India-China border dispute and, 14
Asaphila, India-China border dispute
and, 14
Asia, changing security landscape of,
120–23
Assassinations, 89–90. *See also*
Gandhi, Rajiv
Assured nuclear fuel supply,
negotiations on, 43–44
Asymmetric warfare, use of
deterrence in, 68
Atomic energy. See *entries beginning
"nuclear"*
Atomic Energy Act (U.S., 1954), 36,
42, 44
Atomic Energy Department (DAE),
42, 48, 54
Atomic military revolution, 120–21